CAMBRIDGE LIBRARY COLLECTION

Books of enduring scholarly value

History

The books reissued in this series include accounts of historical events and movements by eye-witnesses and contemporaries, as well as landmark studies that assembled significant source materials or developed new historiographical methods. The series includes work in social, political and military history on a wide range of periods and regions, giving modern scholars ready access to influential publications of the past.

Barrow's Travels in China

William Jardine Proudfoot (*c.*1804–1887) published his critique of Sir John Barrow's *Travels in China* (1804; also reissued in this series) with the agenda of exposing the latter as unreliable and unjust. Barrow had accompanied Lord Macartney on the first British mission to the Chinese Imperial Court (1792–4), in a party that also included the official astronomer, Dr James Dinwiddie, Proudfoot's grandfather. Comparing Barrow's account to that found in other records, Proudfoot concludes that the earlier work was 'a great humbug', ascribing to Barrow the 'powerful motive' of self-promotion. In a work full of vitriol against its subject, Proudfoot's concern is to honour the memory of the mission's members, whom he felt Barrow belittled and vilified, and also to point out factual inaccuracies, accusing him of seeking amusement rather than truth in his anecdotes. Read alongside Barrow's work, it makes for an interesting, scornful, and often entertaining critique.

T0352189

Cambridge University Press has long been a pioneer in the reissuing of out-of-print titles from its own backlist, producing digital reprints of books that are still sought after by scholars and students but could not be reprinted economically using traditional technology. The Cambridge Library Collection extends this activity to a wider range of books which are still of importance to researchers and professionals, either for the source material they contain, or as landmarks in the history of their academic discipline.

Drawing from the world-renowned collections in the Cambridge University Library and other partner libraries, and guided by the advice of experts in each subject area, Cambridge University Press is using state-of-the-art scanning machines in its own Printing House to capture the content of each book selected for inclusion. The files are processed to give a consistently clear, crisp image, and the books finished to the high quality standard for which the Press is recognised around the world. The latest print-on-demand technology ensures that the books will remain available indefinitely, and that orders for single or multiple copies can quickly be supplied.

The Cambridge Library Collection brings back to life books of enduring scholarly value (including out-of-copyright works originally issued by other publishers) across a wide range of disciplines in the humanities and social sciences and in science and technology.

Barrow's Travels in China

WILLIAM JARDINE PROUDFOOT

CAMBRIDGE UNIVERSITY PRESS

Cambridge, New York, Melbourne, Madrid, Cape Town,
Singapore, São Paolo, Delhi, Mexico City

Published in the United States of America by Cambridge University Press, New York

www.cambridge.org
Information on this title: www.cambridge.org/9781108045636

© in this compilation Cambridge University Press 2012

This edition first published 1861
This digitally printed version 2012

ISBN 978-1-108-04563-6 Paperback

'To attempt the discovery of truth is the noblest performance of duty in all men."

"BARROW'S TRAVELS IN CHINA."

AN INVESTIGATION

INTO THE

𝔒rigin and 𝔄uthenticity of the "𝔉acts and 𝔒bservations"

RELATED IN A WORK

ENTITLED "TRAVELS IN CHINA, BY JOHN BARROW, F.R.S."

(AFTERWARDS SIR J. BARROW, BART.)

PRECEDED BY

A PRELIMINARY INQUIRY INTO THE NATURE OF THE "POWERFUL MOTIVE" OF THE SAME AUTHOR,

AND

ITS INFLUENCE ON HIS DUTIES AT THE CHINESE CAPITAL, AS COMPTROLLER TO THE BRITISH EMBASSY, IN 1793.

BY

WILLIAM JARDINE PROUDFOOT

LONDON:
GEORGE PHILIP AND SON, 32, FLEET STREET;
LIVERPOOL: CAXTON BUILDINGS, SOUTH JOHN STREET, AND 51, SOUTH CASTLE STREET.

1861.

PREFACE.

It may seem a perfect supererogation, at this period, to undertake the review of a work published more than half a century ago; a work which was not only noticed by the reviews of the day, but escaped with much honor—in some instances with flying colors. It underwent two successive editions; was printed and circulated in various forms; often largely quoted, and always looked upon as high authority. The author of it ranked among "individuals of acknowledged eminence in science and literature;" and acquired the distinction of a "celebrity of the Georgian era." His devotion to the progress of truth became a universal theme. To this reputation alone the present small volume owes its existence. The writer of it, being in possession of the manuscript journal of a gentleman in the suite of Lord McCartney, ambassador to China, was, unexpectedly, led to look into the work now under notice, when certain strange revelations arrested his attention. This induced him to enter into the history of the information furnished by that mission, and more particularly to an examination of those incidents and occurrences recorded in the *Travels* as "facts and observations," and upon which, as a basis, Chinese society is made to rest. After long and careful application, he has arrived at conclusions widely different from general repute; in a word, he has risen from the task in disgust, and, at once, obeys the call of duty to place the reasons at the bar of public opinion. The object is twofold: justice to the memory of the comptroller's colleagues, on whom the rod of contumely has been laid with an ill grace; and caution to commentators on China respecting the utter folly of adopting the *Travels* as an authority in any case whatever. These objects are to be accomplished by unmasking the hideous forms now covered with the mantle of truth, of which the judges shall decide; and the reviewer rests with conndence on their approval to justify his endeavors.

"We pay truth (observes Sir T. Brown) a very easy compliment when we content ourselves ·with despising her adversaries. The duty we owe her is of a more manly kind: it is to gird ourselves for the battle, to fit us for overcoming those adversaries whenever they shall present themselves in array."

ERRATA.

CONTENTS.

PRELIMINARY INQUIRY.

"Powerful Motive."—Its nature and mode of operation inquired into—illustrated by Lunardi's ascent from Liverpool—truth not its object—ever was at work 13

Claims to Science.—Foundations examined—no early opportunities for information—little progress at the age of 23—science on the embassy not difficult to estimate 16

Do-Nothings of the Embassy.—Contempt manifested for the ambassador's suite—unfit for their duties—execute nothing on the embassy—abilities of the comptroller—his charge of the presents—"large quarto"—great desire of fame 18

"Lot of few to go to Pekin."—Remarkable consequence of this uncommon lot—in two places at the same time—the work of the "powerful motive"—for a purpose 21

Palace of Yuen-Min-Yuen.—Opening of the drama—highly seasoned with incident—unpacking the presents—illustrations of the "motive" . 23

Diodati, interpreter at the palace—his handsome introduction—remarkable disclosure—Latin prohibited to be spoken—ridiculous consequences—ignored by Barrow 25

"Serious Charge."—Ability with which it is conducted—natives astonished at the operations of the "motive"—its unheard-of discoveries—some light thrown on the matter by the erection of the planetarium—residence at the palace not very enviable—only three weeks 26

EMPEROR'S BIRTH-DAY.—Celebration at the palace—incongruous statements of Barrow and Staunton—the former on the horns of a dilemma—statements contrasted with those of Dr. Dinwiddie—begin to look with doubt on the official volumes   29

OLD EUNUCH.—Outburst of ill-feeling—consternation at the palace—reason—Lord McCartney's refusal to perform the Kotoo—contrasted with Dr. Dinwiddie's remarks—the object of the motive—second fiddle .   .   31

OLD EUNUCH.—Alteration of the presents—contradictory statements of Barrow and Staunton—no dependence to be placed on the "Authentic Account."   32

OCTOBER 1ST.—The emperor and the presents—racy extract from the *Auto*—an improvement upon the *Travels*—extracts from Lord McCartney and Dr. Dinwiddie—scientific capacity of the comptroller illustrated by Parker's lens—reasons for supposing the extract from his lordship spurious—desire of the comptroller to get into the presence of the emperor—a curiosity—illustration of the artifice of Sir George Staunton   .   .   34

PARODIES ON LORD MCCARTNEY—illustrating the true character and subsequent success of the comptroller   .   .   .   , ...   40

DISMISSAL OF THE EMBASSY.—Comptroller left behind to settle accounts where none existed—the *Auto* an improvement upon the *Travels*—illustrations of the restraint put upon the embassy—inexplicable movements of the comptroller—despicable account of his farewell ride through the capital—ignores the confusion in being thrust out—concluding remarks   .   41

INVESTIGATION OF "FACTS AND OBSERVATIONS."

SENTIMENTS on the " facts and observations" extracted from the *Travels*   .   47

ECLIPSE AT TONCHOO.—First subject of investigation—proved never to have happened—origin of it—an outrageous plagiarism from the Dutch embassy—the key to unlock the "facts and observations"—little said about the eclipse—reason—the ceremonial of the eclipse compared with the real events of the day—from the *Travels*   48

SCORPIONS AT TONCHOO.—Gross exaggeration to blacken the character of the priests—no dependence on the official details   52

"CANTON ULCER."—Disgraceful fabrication—proved so from the *Travels*—reproduced from Sir George Staunton—observations on reviews   .   54

"FOREIGN DEVILS."—Worthless contradictions—proved so from the facts themselves—origin of the incident   56

"WANT OF FELLOW-FEELING."—Accident at Linsin—grossly misrepresented—

proved so—disgraceful plea put into the mouths of Chinese boatmen—connected with another fallacious occurrence—altogether a texture of inconsistencies 58

INHUMANITY, 1ST ILLUSTRATION.—Punishment of insolent soldier—contradictory statements of Barrow and Staunton—an undoubted fabrication—remarks on reviews 62

INHUMANITY, 2ND ILLUSTRATION.—Cruel and disgraceful treatment of trackers —contradictory statements—not borne out by contemporary witnesses—the whole a detestable whim 64

INHUMANITY, 3RD ILLUSTRATION.—Boatmen on the Pyho unmercifully flogged and cashiered—want of collateral testimony—suspicious extract from Lord McCartney's journal—full of inconsistencies—remarks . . . 68

ILL-TREATMENT OF WOMEN.—Common to see them yolked to a plough—seen only by our author, who knows nothing about it after all—illustrative of disgraceful feelings 70

VESSEL UPSET ON RICE MILL.—Enormous flood—result left to conjecture—ignored and rendered impossible by every other witness—a wanton desire to impose on mankind 72

SPECIMENS OF EXAGGERATION illustrating the capabilities of the " motive"—usually carried to extravagance 74

RASH ASSERTIONS good enough for " facts"—exemplified in describing a typhoon—origin of the "fact" eventually laughed at—no apology for using it 75

POYANG LAKE AND BARROW SWAMPS.—Picture of inconceivable desolation—not quite so bad as painted—confuted by subsequent English embassy—the Barrow swamps not confined to the vicinity of the lake—of indefinite extent—houseless deserts occur where other witnesses see a beautiful cultivated country—Latin and mathematics not necessary to judge of a swamp—accounted for on the principle of astonishing the natives—an improvement upon Sir George Staunton—beauties of the official account in describing these swamps 76

SANDY ISLANDS OF THE POYANG.—Only seen by Sir George Staunton—reasons to doubt his ability, and inquiry into the "fact"—confuted by De Guignes—the islands sailed past by Dr. Milne, and described as hilly and picturesque 80

" SINK OF CHINA."—Name given to the Poyang lake and surrounding swamps—an improvement upon the " Authentic Account"—beautifully illustrating the Barrow-forte. 81

LAKE CINING.—Two absurdities—a country beyond the reach of sight—another with two surfaces—the result of reckless folly—trashy nature of the narrative—observations on Barrow's telescope 82

CONTENTS.

BARROW SWAMPS OF SHANTONG.—Equally extensive and dreary with those of the Poyang—without cultivation and without inhabitants—denied by other witnesses, even by the discoverer himself—jottings from Dr. Dinwiddie's journal respecting the swamps. 84

"IMMENSE AQUEDUCT."—Official and non-official accounts based on the same principle—often wild speculations, never acquired on the embassy—illustrated by the "immense aqueduct"—confuted by the official map—by contemporary and subsequent travellers—by common sense—another marvel amplified from Sir George Staunton 86

GRAND CANAL.—"ALL THE TALENTS"—accounts furnished by the McCartney embassy, deplorable nonsense—proved so by comparing one writer with the other—illustrations of the school in which Barrow was trained . 89

GRAND CANAL—THE COMPTROLLER'S "ENDEAVOR."—Elegance and accuracy of a Barrow sentence—of Chinese geography—wisdom of the "immense aqueduct—looked upon and circulated as "good sense" . . . 91

UNIFORM OF KIANGNAN.—Illustrating the miserable shifts of the McCartney embassy—Barrow-mode of reasoning 94

SOOCHOO BEAUTIES.—Speculations on the ferry girls at Chauchoo, and the ladies at Soochoo—contradictions—further properties of the telescope—elegance of the Barrow-style—drag upon the speculations—rendered impossible by Lord McCartney and other witnesses—Sir George Staunton equally bewildered—reason—bird of paradise 95

LAKE TAIHOO—also reserved for a shot—additional specimens of Sir George Staunton's powers of vision—missionaries and other writers the source of these speculations—disgraceful to the embassy—more reliable information in Anderson than the two able writers 98

TRIFLING NOTABILIA.—Instances overlooked by Sir George Staunton picked up by Barrow—illustrating the grounds where the "facts and observations" were collected 99

SHINGMOO confounded with Poosa—further proofs of a disregard of truth—Lord McCartney's observations on Poosa totally destructive of those of Barrow 100

PARKER'S LENS.—Vacillating statements of Barrow—artifice of Sir George Staunton 102

GARDENS OF YUEN-MIN-YUEN.—Widely different estimates of their content furnished by the "powerful motive"—reason—another plagiarism from the Dutch—splendid illustrations—climax of sophistry—peculiarities of the "facts" 104

PEDESTRIAN FEAT.—Explanatory of contradictions—a thousand miles not less than one-tenth of thirteen hundred miles 106

GLACIS ON GRAND CANAL.—Better views acquired as the distance in time increases—a structure is seen where it never existed—remarkable effort of the "powerful motive"—reflections thereon 107

ACCOMMODATION BAY.—Another beautiful conception of the *Auto*—illustrating ungovernable folly in search of "facts" 108

CHINESE ROADS.—Singular infatuation—the experience of 1793 always improved by subsequent information—no roads in China beyond a foot path—specimen of Barrow reasoning 110

SPECIMENS OF REMARKABLE OBSERVATIONS.—No part of the empire safe from Barrow's telescope 112

CANNON.—All that were seen in China—a few contradictions—Barrow able to form an opinion of their caliber 113

WHIMS ON PECHELEE.—Poverty of the soil and peasantry—worst specimens of humanity seen in all China—remarkable self-contradictions—peasantry happy but not extraordinary happy—reasons—proofs from the Dutch—"interesting remarks" sold at a low figure 114

WASTE LANDS.—Chinese ignorant of reclaiming—richest lands in low, sour, swampy ground—one-fourth part of China lakes and swamps—interior of China not deserts 116

CIVILITIES TO THE EMBASSY.—Cooking in English style—a reproduction from the official volumes—viceroy of Canton travelling post from Pekin—a striking contradiction to Sir George Staunton—tacitly acknowledged by reviewers 117

BARROW'S JOURNAL—a myth—official extracts evidently the work of Sir George Staunton though fathered on Barrow—the Yangtsekiang a reckless miscalculation 119

ENGRAVED REPRESENTATION OF LION—referred to before it was known it would exist 120

AMUSING ANECDOTES of the "Authentic Account" improved on and rendered worthless by Barrow—all evidently fabrications 121

UNASSAILABLE INCIDENTS—demolished by Barrow himself—illustrated by "evening entertainment" on river at Canton—the *Auto* totally demolishes the *Travels* 123

MYSTERIOUS ADVENTURES—illustrated by Linsin pagoda—the Barrow visit demolished by subsequent English embassy—Abel's unable attempt to reconcile the Barrow and Ellis visits 125

PALATIAL INCIDENTS.—Difficult to rebut by external testimony—their incredibility illustrated by the instance of the emperor's favorite draughtsman . 128

BARROW *versus* STAUNTON.

OFFICIAL VOLUMES.—Flattering sentiments thereon—detailed with elegance and accuracy—idle to recapitulate—nevertheless recapitulated and improved on by our author 131

KEETO WHIRLPOOL.—Staunton and Barrow compared—clashing facts—Barrow's account proved a forgery by the official maps—another reproduction, embellished by fabrications 132

CHOLERA MORBUS.—Case at Chusan—Barrow claims to be the victim—remarkable contradictions, Barrow *versus* Staunton, and *versus* himself—case decided by a few facts—Barrow in a ridiculous position—liars and good memories 135

VISIT TO TINGHAI—a texture of inconsistencies—one gentleman ignorant he was stopped every moment to be laughed at—the other that a violent wind nearly upset his palanquin and drove him into a monastery . 137

CHINESE PILOTS.—Each brought a small marine compass according to Staunton —flatly confuted by Barrow—reasons 138

FIRST IMPRESSIONS.—The "unkindest cut"—Barrow persuaded his amiable patron is not telling the truth 139

COUNTRY ON THE PYHO—flat, or not flat—not a hillock to be seen, according to Sir George— broken into hill and dale, according to Barrow—the latter confuted by himself—greater probability and consistency always on the official side 139

SOIL AROUND PEKIN—rich or sterile—rich and highly cultivated, according to Sir George—sterile and unproductive, according to Barrow—the latter again confutes himself—observations on the empty, servile flourishes of the pupil and his contradictions 140

BARROW *versus* THE OFFICIAL MAPS.

GEOGRAPHICAL AND STATISTICAL CONTRADICTIONS.—Testimony of the maps— stamped with the name of Barrow—frequently opposed to the *Travels*— instances previously pointed out—additional instances—all illustrative of the Barrow-school 143

BLUNDERING IN DATES—proof of recklessness and disregard of truth—various instances—remarkable oversight respecting the Cape colony—our author travels all over that colony before he set foot in it 147

BUNGLING.—Interesting specimen from the *Travels*—ships sailing over mountains on dry land 148

LORD McCARTNEY'S JOURNAL.

Bears marks of having been improperly dealt with—various entries pointed out with observations—Parker's lens—boat stranded in the Pyho—illimitable swamps at Cining—dense fog and dismal night on the Lonshiaton—uncivilised people to the southward of Nanyang—this last an anachronism—impossible to have been written by Lord McCartney—peculiarity of the entries—all tending to give a color for certain Barrow whims—his lordship's journal published by Barrow 150

OPPORTUNITIES FOR INFORMATION.

COMPTROLLER never at a loss—quite at home among the Chinese—understands their language, and enjoys a greater share of liberty than his colleagues—real state of things pointed out by extracts from Sir Geo. Staunton and Dr. Dinwiddie—on their arrival, the gentlemen could not understand a word—were afterwards prisoners—passed through the country like so many dumb persons, unable to ask a single question—Barrow's knowledge of the Chinese character a subsequent acquirement 154

RETROSPECT.

INQUIRY FINISHED—black catalogue—their author nevertheless undertakes to correct the errors of other writers—indignation poured out upon Anderson—comparison of the writers—infinitely to the advantage of the humbler individual—list of " vampings" from the *Travels*—second list from do.—challenged to be matched or confuted—a proof of executing something on the embassy—honors in consequence—Edinburgh literati—surprise of the judges—our advice 158

CONCLUSION.

INCONSISTENCIES of the " interesting episode" inexhaustible—idle waste of time to investigate all—observations on the origin of the " Travels in China"—mode of collecting information—introduced in the form of incidents, " facts and observations"—baseless and slippery foundations of some—significance of all—never without a drag—nothing added to the stock of knowledge—summing up of radical and obvious defects—blunders, contradictions, and other fraternities—all pointing to a disregard of truth, and to the animus of the " Travels in China"—opinion of the work by various reviews—our own opinion—conclusion 162

PRELIMINARY INQUIRY.

"POWERFUL MOTIVE."

" It may naturally be supposed," observes Sir John Barrow, in the Preface to the *Autobiography*, " that he who can sit down, in his eighty-third year, to write a volume of five hundred pages, must have been urged on by some powerful motive to undertake such a task, at so advanced a period of life." Although unwilling to confess what this " powerful motive" was, he entertained a pretty clear idea that it would not escape the attention of his readers ; for he observes again, " no man can, with justice, lay vanity to my charge." It would be difficult, indeed, to find another to whom it could with greater justice be applied. If this, however, had been the only cause of complaint silence would have answered every purpose for which this inquiry has been carried out ; but the same " powerful motive," which compelled him to rush into print, has betrayed him into far other improprieties, disgraceful alike to his rank and reputation. Facts fabricated, or misrepresented, admit of no palliation. While we are admonished that the reminiscences of early life are " entirely from memory," we are promised that the record shall be a " true and faithful" one. Let an instance show what reliance is to be placed on this assertion.

B

Immediately on completing his fourteenth year, he entered upon a situation as clerk in an iron-foundry, in Liverpool. We then read : "Not long after my arrival, among the visitors to the manufactory was an Italian, from Naples, of the name of Leonardi, whose business in Liverpool, he told me, was to ascend in a balloon, the first he believed that had been sent up in England, at least with any person in it ; and as his was intended to be inflated with inflammable gas, he wished to know if he could be supplied with iron filings to produce it." (p. 13.) Now, the first ascent of Lunardi, (or Leonardi, as Barrow writes it) from Liverpool, is a historical event, recorded in the annals of the town, and took place July 20th, 1785. As Mr. Barrow was born June 19th, 1764, he had then entered upon his twenty-second year, instead of being a "youth of fourteen," or, at most, fifteen years.

Here then is a material difference which no sophism will reconcile. If our author remembered the event, with the clearness it is attempted to be described, he must have remembered that he had come to manhood, and that he was not the mere boy he endeavors to represent himself. But supposing the panorama of his past existence to have started ever so irregularly into view, it was not only in his power but a very easy matter to have corrected the mistake ; and failing to do so accords ill with a desire to write a " true and faithful " review. It is, at once, a proof that truth was not his object. An honest, and particularly a wise man, would be careful about such matters, even if he had to put himself to trouble, and certainly no less careful when he had no trouble to contend with.

Ambition to have his name, however remote the distance, and however inapplicable, connected with great events seems to have been the sole motive for introducing the story of the balloon, which, unfortunately, introduces too much. When the lady from Liverpool first mentioned the subject of the situation, the memory of our author makes her to say, " From the character I have heard of you, and from age and appearance (perhaps a little too young) I think you would answer our purpose." How is it possible that the lady, who was in search of a youth only, could entertain such an idea, as " perhaps a little too young," when Barrow, at the moment, was not less than twenty years of age.

Again : Sir John's mode of diction would impute to Lunardi much uncertainty on the subject of balloons in England. The very first aeronaut that ever ascended in this country is made to be so far in doubt as to *believe* it was the " first that had been sent up in England, at least with any person in it." Can any man, conversant with the matter, believe that the adventurous Italian was either in doubt, or made use of such language ?

But the whole episode about the balloon is a tissue of egregious falsehoods, among which the would-be aeronaut flounders like a fish on dry land. The ascent from Liverpool is made to follow close upon the declaration of war with France and Spain, and, to keep up appearances, he coolly tells us, " We were, just now, boring up old guns for the merchants, and there were plenty of borings to spare." But what is the fact ? Lunardi's arrival in Liverpool, instead of being near the commencement of the war, was fully two and a half years after peace had been restored.

Such, then, is the manner in which this *apostle of truth and faithfulness* unfolds the particulars of his early life. Historical events are confounded, observations are made, and expressions are put into the mouths of individuals which never could have been entertained, nor uttered, under the circumstances alleged. If events which are really on record be thus treated, what credit can be attached to events and assertions existing only in the autobiographer's memory ?

When Sir John sat down to write his memoirs, he forewarned his readers that he was in his eighty-third year, from which it might be fairly presumed that his faculties were not so clear and vigorous as in the prime of life. The presumption is but reasonable : unfortunately, however, in the course of

this investigation, it will be shown that the same "powerful
motive" *ever was at work*, and that the same disgraceful results
are as conspicuous in the "Travels in China," as they are in
the pet production of his ripe years. Even these memoirs,
though published at so late a period of life, bear internal
evidence of having been long written, but, no doubt, with
occasional improvements, purposely kept back to the last.

FOUNDATION OF CLAIMS TO SCIENCE.

We do not mean to enter minutely into the early life of the
future baronet, but as he, subsequently, takes much credit to
himself for scientific knowledge, it will be found not unprofitable
to glance at the foundation of these claims. From the very
first, we find him studiously underrating his age, evidently to
make his boyhood appear to advantage; and, to assist his
purpose, a few flourishes are introduced which we leave to
biographical compilers, and others who possess sufficient penetration to see their merits. The school which supplied the
rudiments of mathematics was given up at thirteen, and beyond
the little experience gained in the survey of the Priory estate,
and working a few nautical problems, during a voyage to
Greenland, no where do we find this youthful genius engaged
in practical applications of Science, or even cultivating it
abstractedly. He was, in fact, without the books for making
much progress. Still, it is true, he had paid some three or
four visits to the self-taught mathematician of the hills, and
got information on certain points that had "floundered him."
With all this, however, and the oft-repeated assertions about
an inherent and inveterate hatred of idleness, what are we to
think of his acquirements in mathematical science only when,
at the age of twenty-three, he had just learned how to work
the problem of the latitude, and was still ignorant of that of
the longitude : when, moreover, he had but an imperfect know-

ledge of the use of a common set of mathematical drawing instruments. That the few years he shortly afterwards spent in, or near, the metropolis were devoted to good purpose there is reason to believe; but, even then, he was only improving himself as a teacher, and like most other teachers his studies partook of the speculative; for in no one instance do we find him in practical investigations, or applying theory to the common purposes of life.

An estimate, then, may reasonably be formed respecting Mr. Barrow's scientific knowledge at the fortunate period he became the tutor to Sir George Staunton's son, and, through the interest of his patron, placed on the suite of Lord McCartney, ambassador to China. The merit which he assumes to himself in this embassy, and chiefly as a man of science and literature, is the subject of this review: hence our concern for his previous education, of which our readers will be better able to form an opinion from the specimens to be produced, just as they would judge of a tree from the fruit it bears. After making some inquiries into the duties of the comptrollership at the Chinese capital, we will proceed to the investigation of the origin of the numerous incidents, anecdotes, and observations, on the credibility of which a nation's character has been staked. The "Travels in China" are again to be put upon their trial, not in the superficial manner when they first appeared, and by their boldness silenced public opinion into consent; but with a determination to "test rigidly, by weight and measure," the real value of the "facts and observations," which, unfortunately, were too favorably received, and which still continue to exercise their pernicious influence with commentators on the middle kingdom. The witnesses in the case are the manuscript journal alluded to in the Preface, the official and other published accounts of the embassy, including the culprit himself; others occasionally shall be introduced, but only when competent, and such as dare not be disputed. Face to face with these accusers, the *Travels* shall be confronted, and the public, as judge, shall decide whether they stand or fall.

DO-NOTHINGS OF THE EMBASSY.

In pursuing the first part of the inquiry, we shall avail ourselves not only of the *Travels*, but also of the *Autobiography*,
which, besides occasionally clearing away the fog, supplies some
important omissions, which prudence had dictated in the elder
brother. We shall also curtail the name of the younger brother
to its first component, as being less burdensome to the tongue
and ear. As related in the *Auto*, then, the history of the
mission commences with a regulaɪ onslaught on the gentlemen
composing the suite of Lord McCartney, all of whom, with
barely an exception, are deemed unworthy of the duties to which
they were appointed. A little courtesy, surely, would not have
detracted from the merits of the baronet, who names his colleagues with seeming contempt. Instead of giving each his
proper designation in the embassy, he has borrowed the idea
of the "Authentic Account," upon which a significant improvement is made. The Physician to the embassy is turned into
a "Scotch physician;" the Surgeon to the embassy, into a
"naval surgeon;" and so forth; but speaking of himself—he
is "Comptroller of the Household." Consistency is a jewel
which the author of the *Travels* never lays claim to, otherwise
he would have styled himself "an English schoolmaster," or
"a mathematician from Lancashire." But his vanity does not
stop here: he must needs be "John Barrow, Esq.," while
other gentlemen, as respectable in their profession, and
their standing in society, are introduced with the common
prefix, Mr. (*a*)

One gentleman, we are moreover told, "executed nothing
whatever on the embassy;" another—"contributed nothing;"
a third—"supplied a few remarks on the chemistry and medicine of the Chinese;" a fourth—"was expected to instruct the
Chinese in electricity, and in flying balloons, but it all ended
in smoke." Dr. Dinwiddie, the gentleman last alluded to, was
the most popular lecturer on Natural Philosophy at the period,
and owed his appointment in the embassy—not to patronage,

but to his reputation. He was judged to be well qualified to exhibit before the imperial court all the wonders of European science; but other expectations were formed besides these. He had already spent the greater part of thirty years in close connexion with the arts, manufactures, and machinery of the United Kingdom; and had the mission been successful—had opportunities offered for examining those of China, his services were more likely to have been beneficial to the public, at large, than those of the teacher, with all the Latin and mathematics he was master of. (b)

While chastising his colleagues for their remissness, or inability on the embassy, the only really qualified gentleman introduces his own claims to notice with much modesty, thus:

" Mr. Barrow, as Comptroller of the Household, resided five or six weeks at Yuen-min-yuen, to take charge of the valuable presents and see them put in order by the two mechanics, to be presented to the emperor on his return from Tartary, where Lord McCartney had his audience. Mr. Barrow occasionally rode from Yuen-min-yuen to Pekin to look after the property of the embassy left in the large house appropriated to the ambassador and suite in the capital; and on the homeward journey he travelled several hundred miles through the heart of the country, and published a large quarto volume of more than six hundred pages ten years after his return to England."

The value of this " large quarto" will be attended to in good time; in passing, however, we may observe how ready its author is to impress the reader with an idea of its magnitude— " more than six hundred pages!" The quality, no doubt, is to be presumed from the quantity, which exhibits an approach to the truth never found in the volume itself; even the bulk of the *Auto*, another object of self-congratulation, is stated within its true limits. As to the other something, however, taking " charge of the valuable presents "—it is a disingenuous flourish. The comptroller here arrogates to himself the entire merit of a transaction which, in its most favorable aspect, was only a partnership: that is—the fitting up of the presents in the palace of Yuen-min-yuen. He and the two mechanics did it! not a word of Dr. Dinwiddie, who nevertheless can be shown not only to have had something to do in the matter, but to have spent more time attending to it than any other person. These presents, it will be remembered, consisted of two classes : one, beautiful specimens of English art and manufacture ; the other, costly scientific machines : the former fell to the charge of the comptroller ; the latter to that of Dr. Dinwiddie, who was the only gentleman competent. Some light will be thrown on this by and bye ; in the meantime, his designation, " Machinist to the embassy," is significant enough ; while Anderson, who could only reflect the sentiments of the period, and particularly those around him, adds " Conductor of mathematical and astronomical presents," all of which is fully borne out by the doctor's journal, now in the reviewer's possession. Sir George Staunton, in his usual sophisticated style, instead of giving a proper list of the gentlemen, names only a part, and seems more desirous of confounding than explaining the designation by which each was attached to the embassy. But to be brief with this fitting up business : on the 23rd August, the second day after the arrival of the embassy at head quarters, and before a single article was unpacked, Dr. Dinwiddie (not Mr. Barrow) accompanied Lord McCartney and Sir George Staunton, on their very first visit, to the palace, expressly to attend the consultation about the disposal of these machines and the other presents. The business was settled there and then, in the absence of the comptroller. If he had been the person he represents himself he would, on this occasion, have been consulted in preference to Dr. Dinwiddie, who, it is evident, was the principal in the business.

Our readers, we trust, will pardon this digression in a matter of no other importance beyond interposing a check to the insatiable consequence of the comptroller, who is not over scrupulous as to how he earns his meed of praise. Not content with squeezing merit out of a transaction that had little to boast of, he is even willing to take the entire responsibility upon himself, to show that he executed something on the embassy. This desire of praise is truly manifest throughout the *Auto*, where, from beginning to end, the pile acquires such gigantic proportions as to stagger the beholder in looking up at it. Not one iota of merit is wasted, and no Australian digger was ever half so anxious of the shining, scattered spangles, as the successful baronet about his future fame. We sincerely congratulate him on so laudable an ambition, and, while we do so, promise that no exertions on our part shall be wanting to render it as perfect as possible.

"LOT OF FEW TO GO TO PEKIN."

From the title page of the *Travels*, we learn "It is the lot of few to go to Pekin," and truly the motto has been turned to good account. Sheltered behind its ample shield, such unwarranted liberties have been taken with the proceedings of the embassy, that we look in vain for even *one* circumstance being related as it really happened. Confusion is made the order of the day, and the narrative, in consequence, to ignore, misrepresent, and confound. No sooner is the *uncommon lot* accomplished, and our enviable traveller safe at the further end of his memorable journey, than he commits himself, so far as to occupy two distant places at the same time. After a short-lived residence of five days at the villa of Hung-ya-yuen, the embassy was removed to more spacious apartments in the capital, and our author endeavors to place himself in the returning cavalcade, on this occasion, when he had taken up his abode, and was assisting at the palace of Yuen-min-yuen. At page 103 of the *Travels*, we read: "On returning to the capital, we passed through the great street of a town called Hatien," &c., giving the particulars of the journey. Now, Mr. Barrow could not have disputed the edition he published of Lord McCartney's journal, wherein it is stated, "August 24, Sir George Staunton went to Yuen-min-yuen, and took with him Mr. Barrow, Dr. Dinwiddie, Thibault, and Petit-Pierre, to give them instructions about arranging the machinery," &c. "These gentlemen are to remain, for this purpose, at Yuen-min-yuen." Again : neither could Mr. Barrow dispute his own *Travels*, wherein he tells us : "The three first days, while the articles were unpacking and assorting, we remained tolerably quiet," &c. Now, it so happens, it was during these three first days that the embassy moved from Hung-ya-yuen into Pekin. Thus John Barrow, Esq., a fellow of the Royal Society, has the assurance to place himself in the returning cavalcade, at the same time he knew he was, and admits being busy at the imperial palace. To attend personally on two distant duties is laying claim to an important office, and shows a very willing disposition to execute something on the embassy. But that our readers may not have the shadow of a doubt in this matter, we find the two extracts, last quoted, positively confirmed by our manuscript journal. "August 25. All the suite, except Mr. Barrow and myself, and two workmen, set out to-morrow morning for Pekin ; we are to lodge in the palace, and to remain here till all be finished." The same authority also informs us that Mr. Barrow made his first return visit to Pekin on the 28th ; and this is confirmed, to the very letter, by his lordship observing, "August 28, Mr. Barrow returned from the palace, and said they had put up Parker's two lustres," &c., all this demonstrating, in the most conclusive manner, that the comptroller was at the palace on the 26th August, and not with the embassy returning to Pekin.

The *Auto* has already informed us that its author writes partly from memory, and partly from "loose notes," written fifty years ago. This doubtless is the truth, and seems about the only sentence, in these volumes, on which we can with confidence rely. Lord McCartney, speaking of notes written on the ground of recollection, observes : "They are apt to vary their hue considerably." Mr. Barrow's notes illustrates this in a peculiar manner ; not only has the hue varied considerably, but the very objects, themselves, have changed into totally different shapes. It was, however, out of his power, in this instance, either from "loose notes," or from recollection, to have penned the paragraph at page 103 of the *Travels*. To some, the circumstance may seem immaterial, but it is not so; because it is the work of the "powerful motive"—it is a fabrication, and there was a purpose for it. By this ridiculous arrangement of the narrative, our author contrives to make it appear he only went to the palace at the same time the ambassador started for Tartary. To use one of his favorite quotations, he had too many "fantastic tricks to play" at Yuen-min-yuen to admit any other to share in the glory, and, of course, he is careful to have his superiors out of the way before he begins. Had he acknowledged his introduction by Sir George Staunton and the interpreter, his cap would have lost some of its brightest feathers, and to preserve these feathers he ignores their assistance, and endeavors to mislead his readers by appearing in the cavalcade, on its return to Pekin.

PALACE AT YUEN-MIN-YUEN.—Opening of the Drama.

In this manner, then, the *uncommon lot* of going to Pekin begins to unfold itself, presenting a foretaste of the disorder into which the proceedings must, of necessity, be thrown. We have, however, traced the enviable gentleman to the imperial palace, where a few weeks residence is magnified into a momentous concern. As a correct statement of the transactions there would be "flat, stale, and unprofitable," he has, by the aid of the "powerful motive," contrived to season it with innumerable incidents, and other particulars, by which, as a matter of course, he appears a very important personage; in short, as the only entity about Yuen-min-yuen. At the risk of being deemed prolix and devoid of interest, we proceed to overhaul some of these pretensions, believing it to be of importance to be able to form a just estimate of any statement advanced by an author of reputation.

As already shown, by the qutoation from his lordship, Mr. Barrow, on his first arrival at the palace, was accompanied not only by Dr. Dinwiddie and the workmen, but also by Sir George Staunton and the interpreter, who came expressly to see the work begun, and to make the necessary arrangements for those who were to remain. Resolved on having nothing to do with such an introduction, the comptroller, like a hero alone in his glory, makes his *debut* in the grand drama he is about to perform, and finds, to his great alarm, " a number of Chinese workmen busily employed in breaking open the packages, some in one place and some in another, to the no little danger of the globes, clocks, glass lustres, and such like frangible articles," &c. (p. 106.) Instead of our hero, Lord McCartney mentions the interpreter detecting some such intermeddling; it cannot, however, be gathered from Dr. Dinwiddie's journal that there was any such danger on the part of the Chinese, although there was on the part of the minister-plenipotentiary himself, who did not think it beneath his dignity to dash at the contents of a case, which he opened with "impatience." Mr. Barrow, who is ignorant of such a gentleman being present, would never see his patron engaged in such a pastime, although he was sharp enough to see the Chinese. He is equally sharp in ascertaining "that not a single article was either missing or injured," notwithstanding a pane of curved glass, in the dome of the planetarium, was rendered useless by a crack. This injured pane figures conspicuously in the illustrations, not only of Sir George Staunton and Lord McCartney, but of the very individual who now denies that such an injury existed; (p. 306) and trifling as the circumstance may appear, it is exactly characteristic of our author, who risks assertions regardless of their foundations, or the consequences to which they lead. Such trifles, too, are scattered so profusely throughout the " large quarto " that, to borrow an idea from a celebrated artist, they accumulate till they become *no trifle*.

DIODATI AND THE LATIN LANGUAGE.

Having despatched a multiplicity of business, a gentleman appeared, " who, notwithstanding his Chinese dress, I soon perceived to be an European. He introduced himself by saying, in the Latin language, that his name was Deodato, a Neapolitan missionary, and that the court had appointed him to act as interpreter; hoped he might be useful to us, and offered his services in the most handsome manner," &c., (p. 107.)

This missionary had already been seen by the gentlemen of the embassy, having, on the previous day, been to the ambassador's lodgings, and also the interpreter when the consultation was held about fitting up the presents. He had now come to meet Sir George Staunton and Mr. Plumb, the interpreter to the embassy, respecting the accommodations at the palace, as already stated. To suppose, then, that it required any intuitive faculty in the comptroller to " perceive " that Diodati was " an European," or that Diodati would introduce himself in the " most handsome manner," is simply ridiculous. But our hero of the palace, who is never at a loss for noble qualities in his chiefs, never lets a syllable with an opposite tendency escape him; of course, he studiously avoids mention of every thing upon which they had set their veto. It so happens, then, that a most remarkable circumstance, bearing upon this pretended interview with Diodati, remains to be told. However ignored by the comptroller, it is, nevertheless, a fact that the gentlemen of the embassy, for a length of time, were not allowed to hold any conversation whatever with the missionaries : Latin, being the only medium of discourse, was strictly forbidden to be spoken at all. Whether the policy was good or bad is, at present, immaterial ; it is enough that the prohibition existed, and, in consequence, some scenes bordering on the ridiculous took place. " One father addressed Dr. Gillan, ' Tu loquaris Latinum, Domine ?' Mum ! Learned Doctors not speak Latin ! " exclaims our informant, startled, no doubt, at the ideas the missionaries would naturally conjure up. Even Sir

George Staunton once, in the presence of Diodati, so far forgot himself as to make use of a Latin quotation to some of the gentlemen.   The prohibition was eventually removed, and the gentlemen allowed to converse with the missionaries in a lan-guage which they (the gentlemen) did not previously under-stand ; it was not, however, till the ambassador started for Tartary.   Only the day before, and eight days after the party had been set to work, Dr. Dinwiddie, at the palace, received from Sir George Staunton, in Pekin, a letter strictly forbidding any one at the palace to speak Latin, even to Diodati, the very man who brought the letter, and who handed it to the doctor, with a significant glance at the seal, bearing the motto, *Fiat Responsio*.

After this, a tolerable idea may be conceived of the "most handsome manner" in which Diodati introduced himself : indeed, it might seem superfluous to waste any further time on the palatial drama of the comptroller, as the position in which he was placed, by the prohibition, rendered any attempts at consequence an absurdity.   However, we do not rely on this circumstance alone, and the reader will find that though ignored both by Sir George Staunton and his pupil they do not always show the same wisdom.   Each is too eager, by half, to encourage the growth of his own favorite offspring, scarcely stopping short of any thing in the shape of food ; and where-ever the former clears the way the latter is sure to rush after, splashing the mud about, even in his master's face.

TRANSACTIONS AT YUEN-MIN-YUEN.

SERIOUS CHARGE.

At the palace, we find the comptroller settling, in dashing style, the matter of the lodgings, notwithstanding it had been done by the interpreter.   We find his charge became "serious" when "surrounded by the Tribunal of Mathematics, and other learned persons, all asking questions concerning astronomy and mathematics ; " attending, curiously enough, to certain duties that also fell to the lot of Dr. Dinwiddie. We again find some of these persons so stupid as to fancy a man with such a charge could not "possibly have any knowledge of the astronomical instruments, after professing his ignorance in *casting a nativity.*" But more remarkable, we find the emperor's favorite draughts-man, an individual only known to Mr. Barrow, employed in executing drawings of the "grand machines;" and that the attempts of such an eminent personage proved "preposterous," till our superintendent took the pencil in hand, and rendered them ship-shape. Equally mysterious, we find our hero in the presence of a "great number of Tartar generals, and military officers," who are struck with amazement at beholding solid bars of iron cut asunder by the blade of a sword, without injuring its edge. We, moreover, find him exhuming an "enormous large scorpion," which had found its way, through impossibilities, into the middle of a case of Birmingham ware. Thus, ever and anon, the "powerful motive" is astonishing the natives by its superior force ; or it finds itself astonished in return by wonderful discoveries, which never reached the ears of another individual on the embassy. In short, the responsibility of the charge, and the ability with which it was conducted, can only be appreciated by a thorough investigation of the overgrown "quarto," and such of our readers as have not paid attention to this, will form but a feeble outline of the eventful history now transpiring at Yuen-min-yuen. Some of the most curious of these adventures are with the old eunuch, the keeper of the palace, respecting whom, and his train, we have some observations to offer, as they throw a little light upon the proceedings at this imperial residence. In accom-plishing their task, the fitting-up party experienced the greatest annoyance from these characters, although Sir John asserts he "soon put a stop to their officious intermeddling in matters that did not concern them." Among other entries on this subject, our journal furnishes the following, when about to remove into Pekin.

"September 14. This day, finished the planetarium. It

has been a troublesome job, not owing to any difficulty in the
work, but the inconvenience arising from a number of imper-
tinent eunuchs, keepers of the palace, who made so much noise,
and what they thought fun, that it was frequently impossible
to attend to the business. The planetarium will, by this mode
of erecting, lose much of its effect. An ignorant people should
be taken by surprise. When a grand machine is shown all at
once, and the principles of motion concealed, it seldom fails in
its effect; but when it is shown piecemeal, when the various
detached parts are exhibited, and put together in their sight;
in short, when the machine is built from its foundation before
them, the time seems long; they impute every trifling mistake,
or hesitation of the workman about placing this or that part,
which can be known, most frequently, only by trial, to a want
of knowledge in the machine, and want of ability in the profession. For example : when the platform was laying, and it
became necessary to select such and such pieces, as belonged
to such and such parts, which, together with making all fast
and level, took up a good deal of time—the men were told,
they labored much and did nothing. From all which, I am of
opinion that the machine is much lowered in the estimation of
the people about the palace; and that the prejudices entertained by the Chinese, respecting the ingenuity and address
of our workmen, will be confirmed. I gave it as my opinion,
long before our arrival in the country, that not only the
planetarium, but all the other presents, should be properly
fitted up before they were seen by any one, even by the mandarines, if possible, and experience has now convinced me of
the propriety of that opinion."

This presents no very pleasing picture of the residence
enjoyed by the gentlemen at Yuen-min-yuen. If the hero of
a thousand adventures ever "put a stop" to the officious
intermeddling of the eunuchs, it must have been of very short
duration, no longer than his back was turned; for we have the
same proof it continued, more or less, from first to last. But
what occasion is there for proof? Is it reasonable to suppose

that John Barrow, Esq., though dignified by the appellation of a comptroller, in the British embassy, could exercise any control over those who held him in honorable imprisonment ? It is not reasonable, and his own whims will yet bear witness against him.

But besides being annoyed and laughed at, his residence turns out to have been of much shorter duration than asserted by the *Auto*, which fixes the period at five or six weeks, as if there could be any room for a doubt. We have already shown that the party took up their abode on the 24th of August, and we quote again : " Sunday, September 15. This day, at 11, Mr. Barrow, Thibault, and Petit-Pierre, set off, with their and my baggage, to Pekin." Nothing can be more satisfactory than this, which fixes, to a day, the period of the comptroller's residence. Including his visits to Pekin, once or twice a week, it amounts only to three weeks. After the fitting-up party had removed into the capital, Dr. Dinwiddie's attendance was still necessary at the palace, which he visited almost daily, chiefly on account of the planetarium, whose complicated motions had to be regulated to a great nicety. The three weeks, then, together with two or three visits about the time of the emperor's return from Tartary, constitute the sum total of the comptroller's residence at this imperial palace ; however, as he positively refuses to give up possession, till compelled by the dismissal of the embassy, we intend humouring him to satisfy our readers whether it redounds to his credit.

EMPEROR'S BIRTH-DAY.

" On the 17th, being the emperor's birth-day, all the princes and officers about the palace assembled in their robes of ceremony, to make their obeisance to the throne in the great hall of audience." And further on, " The old eunuch told me that I might remain in the hall during the ceremony, if I would consent to perform it with them, and offered to instruct me in it." (p. 116.

On certain conditions, the comptroller is here allowed to witness a certain ceremony, but, strangely enough, does not say that he accepted of those conditions, or even that he was present, and witnessed the ceremony; still, he is desirous to impress his readers with the idea that he was present, and saw all that went on. This ambiguous style is one of the most remarkable peculiarities of our author, who is continually thrusting in a story, about something or other, without finishing it. Sir George Staunton, however, clears up the matter so far as to affirm that Mr. Barrow was present on the occasion. (II, p. 303.) In consequence, the comptroller is placed on the horns of a dilemma; for, according to his own words, the price of his admission was the performance of the very prostrations he takes such credit to himself for indignantly refusing on all other occasions. The position is most ridiculous; if he remained in the hall, he performed the conditions; if he did not remain in, he makes Sir George Staunton anything but a gentleman. The author of the *Travels* is welcome to either horn. Such disingenuous notices of a transaction that involved no cause for it, would disgust any man of veracity, but it is the predominant feature of the school to which the "two able writers" belong. A few general observations, picked up anyhow, are moulded anew, so as to assume the appearance of a reality actually transpiring before their eyes; but unable to give a proper account, the transaction naturally becomes involved in a mist.

But, in this instance, we are in possession of a mode of clearing away the mist, and proving the whole affair a trumped up story, from the first, to assist in embellishing the "Authentic Account," the details of which are so elegant and so accurate. It shows how difficult it is to steer clear of rocks when truth is thrown overboard; and furnishes a beautiful illustration of the maxim, "Truth tells best." All this is manifest from the writers themselves, but confirmed from Dr. Dinwiddie's journal, which shows that none of the gentlemen had that day (Sept. 17) been to the palace. Mr. Barrow

and the workmen had removed, with their baggage, on the
15th; the doctor followed the next day, and on the 17th they
are all immured in the ambassador's hotel, in Pekin, each
attending to his own private affairs. There is not the shadow
of a doubt that the ceremony, here alluded to, is fabricated from
a similar occurrence on the 8th, the occasion of the new moon.
This also took place before the throne; and so far from either
joining therein, or being shut out, the gentlemen, in the hall,
looked on, or pursued their work unmolested all the time.
Whatever the man of the *uncommon lot* is interested in, must
naturally have a corresponding character—tremendous, terrific,
bold, grand, or stately—none of your common affairs; and so
the mere occasion of the new moon would not, in such chivalrous
eyes, appear of equal importance with the birth-day of the
emperor. From this circumstance, we begin to look with dis-
trust on the veracity even of the "Authentic Account."

OLD EUNUCH—OUTBURST OF ILL-HUMOUR.

This birth-day is a period of stirring events. Only two days
after, September 19, " On going as usual in the morning to the
hall of audience, I found the doors shut, and the old eunuch,
who kept the keys, walking about in so sullen a mood that I
could not get from him a single word. Different groups of
officers were assembled in the court-yard, all looking as if
something very dreadful either had occurred, or was about to
happen. Nobody would speak to me, nor could I get the least
explanation of this extraordinary conduct, till at length our
friend Deodato appeared with a countenance no less woful than
those of the officers of government, and the old eunuch. I
asked him what was the matter? His answer was, we are all
lost, ruined, and undone!" (p. 117.)

The missionary, here, explains how Lord McCartney had
refused to comply with the usual ceremony of prostration, and
that direful consequences were likely to be the result. All

this, and a great deal more, we learn from the keen observer of passing events ; but there is great room to doubt if any of the gentlemen visited the palace on this day, September 19. Dr. Dinwiddie did not, and the others had no duties to attend to. One thing, however, is certain, Diodati was not there : he had gone to his imperial majesty, in Tartary, with a description of the orrery, so as to compare it with another machine in the royal residence, at Gehol. And further, Diodati did not make his appearance again at the palace of Yuen-min-yuen till the emperor's return. So much for the missionary. But this blazing fit of ill-humour is entirely unknown to the gentleman who, of all others, was the most likely to have experienced its effects, as none spent so much time at the palace, and none was more alive to the news from Gehol. A keen penetration is not necessary to reach the bottom of this speculation. The comptroller looks upon himself as a *little ambassador*, and, in consequence, is encountering the same trials, and the same successes of his lordship, to whom he is actually paying his compliments in the character of second fiddle. This will appear more evident in the course of a few pages. In passing, we may observe that it is the *Travels* which fixes this event on the 19th September, but that the *Auto* fixes it on the 16th, showing, among other matters, the blundering stupidity in arranging dates.

OLD EUNUCH AND THE PRESENTS.

Still harping on the vicious conduct of the old eunuch, on this occasion, we learn that he " conceived, as he thought, a notable piece of revenge. Some pains had been taken to arrange the presents in such a manner in the great hall as to fill the room well, and set them off to the best advantage. The old creature, determined to give us additional trouble, and to break through the arrangement that had been made, desired that the whole might be placed at one end of the room. On my objecting to this he pretended to have received the emperor's order, and that at all events it must be obeyed." (p. 233.)

What an idea of revenge! because his lordship, at Gehol, refuses to comply with the ceremony of the Ko too, the old eunuch, at Yuen-min-yuen, orders the machines to be shifted about. Whether does this circumstance prove the eunuch, or the comptroller, to have been the master at the palace? We believe the latter gentleman has signally committed himself in asserting he "put a stop" to the old creature's officiousness. Surely, if the comptroller exercised any control now was his opportunity; and possibly he did, only, Barrow-like, he leaves us to infer: it would be making his readers too wise to let them know if the alteration ever took place. Sir George Staunton, however, again steps in, and puts the matter beyond a doubt, in the affirmative: "Three days before, and three days after, the emperor's birth-day," being devoted to this purpose, according to the official account. (II, p. 320.) Now, mark the clash of assertion! If the "Authentic Account" deserves the credit of *Authentic*, the change must have been conceived on, or before, the 14th September, and, therefore, could *not* be a "notable piece of revenge" resulting from the news of the 19th. It is quite evident, Sir George Staunton had no idea that the alteration at Yuen-min-yuen resulted from his lordship's refusal at Gehol; and, we believe, no other writer but the author of the *Travels* could have hit on such a cause for it. · However, it is one of the numerous instances where we find the pupil following in the wake of his master, and dashing, with impatience, to the same feast, which he looks upon as common property; but, while gorging his *own beauty*, he seems unconscious, or rather reckless, that he is, at the same time, bespattering the *beauty of his benefactor*.

But again: the period devoted by Sir George Staunton, to this alteration, turns out to be preposterous when tested by the journal of Dr. Dinwiddie, who knew all that was transpiring at the palace, as well as Mr. Barrow, and who could not, possibly, have avoided mention of a circumstance in which he was so much mixed up. Instead of shifting the planetarium, he was all the while regulating its movements. Still, without assigning any reason, he simply observes that the orrery, the globes, the clocks, and the lustres, were " moved ; " an operation that did not require even one whole day, instead of the six or seven mentioned by the minister-plenipotentiary. This circumstance is indicative of the comptroller's charge being an easy matter after all.

OCTOBER FIRST—EMPEROR AND THE PRESENTS —PARKER'S LENS, &c.

From first to last, Mr. Barrow deserves credit for his struggles in supporting the character he has chosen at Yuen-min-yuen, and at no period is it better represented than on the emperor's return from Tartary. He is not only face to face, when the emperor inspected the presents, but has the singular felicity to find his labours approved of, and himself the object of the emperor's munificence. The whole paragraph is so racy that we give it entire, from the *Auto*, only intimating that, with one exception, it is substantially a re-print from the *Travels.*

" The following day, the 1st October, the emperor, attended by a Tartar prince, inspected the presents in the hall of audience, and examined many of them more attentively than I could have imagined. He desired the Tartar prince to tell us, through Deodato, that the accounts he had received of our good conduct at Yuen-min-yuen had given him great pleasure, and that he had ordered a present to be made to each of us as a proof of his entire satisfaction. The present consisted of rolls of silk, and pieces of silver cast in the form of a Tartar shoe, each being about an ounce in weight. They were delivered by the old eunuch, who wished to exact from us the usual prostrations, even after the emperor had departed ; but I only laughed at him, and asked him where the bamboos were kept ; he understood me, gave a grin and a growl, and walked away. I thought it right, however, to desire Deodato to explain to the Tartar prince, who remained, that we had no objection to do as the ambassador had done at Gehol, and which had been repeated by us on meeting the emperor ; and he immediately said nothing more was required. Accordingly, on receiving the presents, we each placed one knee on the lowest step leading to the throne. I told Lord McCartney what we had done, and he said it was perfectly correct." (p. 84.)

The exception alluded to, just previous to commencing the extract, is when the old eunuch wished to exact the usual prostrations. In the *Travels*, our author " made him no answer," and, of course, never " asked him where the bamboos were kept." (p. 121.) This incident, then, suggested itself some forty years afterwards, and was, no doubt, considered as an improvement, worthy the last edition of so " interesting an episode" as the Chinese mission. But we will undertake to show that not only this exception, but the whole paragraph is a perfect rodomontade, disgraceful to its author. However, before we proceed further, we shall introduce another extract, this time from Lord McCartney's journal, premising that it was published by Mr. Barrow, who wrote his lordship's life.

" Tuesday, October 1. The gentlemen and artists, at Yuen-min-yuen, returned to finish that business, and put up Parker's great lens, which I had procured from Captain McIntosh, and which seemed to strike the Chinese in a peculiar manner ; and yet so ignorant are they, in matters of this kind, that they asked Mr. Barrow whether he could not make such another for them, and when he told them, it was made by the artist who had executed the lustres, and whose sole profession was to compose works of glass and crystal, and that there was not such another lens in the world besides, they shook their heads as if they doubted his veracity; but having asked Dr. Gillan the same question apart, and receiving a similar answer, they appeared to be somewhat satisfied. They, however, requested that it might be fixed in its place

immediately; and when they were informed that it would require
some time, they expressed the utmost astonishment, and were
scarcely made to comprehend how it could admit of any delay,
as they said it was the emperor's order to have it done
instantly, for he was impatient to see it, and our gentlemen
might have 100, 200, or any number of hands that they
choose to call for to assist them. The legate indeed, testified no
less surprise, on a former occasion, on being told that it would
take several weeks to combine all the several movements of the
planetarium, imagining that labor, not skill, was the only thing
necessary, and that putting together so complicated a
machine, as a system of the universe, was an operation as
easy and simple as the winding-up of a jack."

Now, with perhaps the sentiment embodied in the first four
lines, or so, the whole of the foregoing paragraph will be
shown to carry the stamp of a forgery, foisted into his lordship's
journal; in the mean time, it is evidence of Messrs. Gillan and
Barrow having something to do with the great lens, upon this
day, in proof of which we are about to place another gentleman
in the witness box. Mr. Barrow, who scatters his dates about,
sometimes at random, and sometimes as he finds convenient,
is at least correct in naming October 1st, as the day following
the emperor's return from Tartary. To show, therefore, what
was really transpiring on that day, as well as to show how
competent the comptroller was to take charge of the
scientific instruments he makes so much parade about, we
subjoin another extract from the manuscript journal already
frequently quoted. It will, however, be well to acquaint the
reader that a portion of the presents, including Parker's lens,
Herschell's telescope, the air pump, and the mechanical
powers, were sent from Pekin to the palace only two days
before the emperor's arrival; and that these machines were not
placed in the hall of audience, but in a different hall, entirely
separated from it. The lens at the time was still unpacked,
although we are told "they were all perfectly ready." By
publishing the journal of his lordship, the comptroller has, in

reality, committed himself on this point: but to our private record.

"Tuesday, October 1. Dr. Gillan, Mr. Barrow, and the workmen, set off for Yuen-min-yuen, as they said, to pack up the carriages; I learned it was to put up the lens. Sir George, on my application, procured a carriage, and Lord McCartney, Sir George, Mr. Plumb, and I, set out for the palace. My lord's object was to get some letters, which the colao had received from Chusan. The letters had been opened, and Diodati called on to read one, but being in English, he could not. I went to the hall, where I found Gillan and Barrow in a great bustle, attempting to erect the house for the lens. Dr. Gillan, who undertook the business, did not remember a single circumstance respecting the putting up of the house. He and Barrow went to town: I remained with the workmen."

Here, then, Dr. Dinwiddie, who had every opportunity of knowing what was transpiring, never alludes to a single circumstance as related by the comptroller on this eventful October 1st; and he must have gone immeasurably out of his way, forming, as he did, one of the party at the palace whose good conduct had so pleased the emperor. Instead of these nonsensical flourishes, other circumstances had been transpiring, not very creditable to the scientific knowledge of Mr. Barrow, who keeps ringing the changes in our ears. Under cover of another object, he and Dr. Gillan started to "astonish the natives," but, finding themselves astonished, had to back out of their indiscretion, and return to town. The main features, indeed, are substantially borne out by the suspicious extract from Lord McCartney: it confirms the visit of the two gentlemen to Yuen-min-yuen, their object, and the difficulties attending their officious endeavours to erect the house. On comparing the extracts, the reader must be forcibly struck with the ostentation assumed in that from his lordship; of the introduction of the names of Barrow and Gillan, and the total silence of the only individual who could, and did exhibit the powers of this wonderful apparatus. Nothing short of unblushing impudence could have dictated the paragraph in question, whether entered with his lordship's consent or not. It is not, however, in his lordship's style, which is always clear, and free from hobbling periods; but in the interminable, ambiguous, and self-conceited style of the gentleman who gave it to the world. If there were no other proof, the round-about answer, to the plain question of the Chinese, would be enough; but it is also curious that the entry should wind up with a simile on the planetarium in nearly the same observations furnished by the *Travels* on the same machine ; a co-incidence curious indeed. It is still further curious that the visit of his lordship, to Yuen-min-yuen, for the Chusan letters, and which should have been inserted on this day, is postponed to the day following; no doubt to make room for the ostentatious paragraph under notice. But a still stronger suspicion is to be found in the fact that his lordship, at Pekin, should the first thing this day enter into his journal a transaction occurring some seven or eight miles away. If he could, possibly, have made the entry upon the very day, it must have been by Gillan and Barrow returning with the news, and, consequently, adding another confirmation to the truth from our manuscript. Beyond all doubt, the entry is an after consideration, whether sanctioned by authority or not.

But other considerations militate against the disputed extract, which reads with an ill grace after the spicy proceedings in the hall of audience, where the fitting-up party were so highly complimented for good conduct. If the presents were all perfectly ready, how is it that the lens-house was still unpacked, and " that it would require some time" to be fixed in its place ? The truth is, Sir John is too hurried to bring himself into contact with the Chinese potentate, and, this eventful day being the first opportunity, his impatience becomes ungovernable; he rushes into the hall of audience, meets his majesty, and presents the world with his version of "Much ado about nothing." An explanation of all this may be derived from the fact that, on his return to Ulverstone, they looked upon him, who had been to Pekin and seen the emperor, as a *great curiosity*, "which, indeed, I seemed to be," he adds, innocently enough. But it is extremely doubtful if he ever saw the emperor beyond a mere glance into a sedan chair, when the embassy met the imperial procession returning from Tartary. Not a single circumstance favors the idea that he did. It appears evident, the fitting up party were not admitted into the hall of audience after the emperor's return; and as to the inspection of the presents there, his majesty was impatient to see them, and his curiosity was satisfied immediately on his arrival, when every individual of the embassy, without exception, was either on the way to, or already safely immured in the ambassador's lodgings in Pekin. For the three following days, to the evening of October 3rd, Dr. Dinwiddie and the workmen remained at the palace, but confined to that hall where the lens, telescope, air-pumps, and mechanical powers were set up; on all of which he wrought the only experiments, and delivered the only lectures, that were attempted. These were attended by the state ministers, and Diodati, as interpreter. When properly adjusted, the lens-house was honored by a royal visit; but, so far from being examined with minute attention, his imperial majesty looked at the apparatus not more than *two minutes*, and retired. This was on the 2nd, apparently in the comptroller's absence; at all events, the party present, including the doctor and workmen, were conducted to a private corner to be out of the way.

Regarding the emperor's inspection of the presents, Sir George Staunton, himself, labours to convey a very erroneous impression. Assuming a little of the Gibbonian style, he writes, "Several of the instruments and machines were tried in his presence; distant objects were observed through the telescopes; and metals melted in the focus of Parker's great lens." (II, p. 324.) In this showy manner, the emperor, on the very day of his return, is welcomed to Yuen-min-yuen, although there was not a single gentleman of the embassy

present to perform experiments. Parker's lens, as shown, was
not even unpacked ; but after it was put up, the emperor
never saw it tried. The experiment of melting the *Chinese
cash* was done by Dr. Dinwiddie, on the 3rd, in presence of
the state officers, including the prime minister, who lighted
his pipe at the focus of the lens, in derision of its usefulness.
He wished, indeed, to know how an enemy's town could be
set on fire by it, and how it was to act in a cloudy day. But
this and other experiments were accompanied by such contempt
and ill humour, that the party were glad, that evening, to get
away to their prison - home in Pekin. To confirm the state of
feeling manifested by the Chinese, at this juncture, it was
discovered next morning, (October 4th,) that the glass lustres
had been taken down and moved away ; that the lens-house,
too, was in pieces, and the two lenses lying on the pavement ;
besides other of the instruments thrown aside in disorder as
useless ; *all by the emperor's command.* This was the last day
any of the suite saw the palace. Such, then, was the real
opinion of the Chinese court respecting this great instrument,
which was *never* tried in his majesty's presence. This Sir
George Staunton well knew.

PARODIES ON LORD McCARTNEY.

The same motive that ushered the comptroller into the
presence of his majesty, would naturally squeeze some parade
out of the presents, which were neither delivered in the hall
of audience, nor particularly for the purpose stated : the royal
munificence, indeed, extended to the whole train, even to the
meanest servant. The ceremonial in which the old eunuch is
threatened with the bamboo, is evidently a play upon his
lordship's success at Gehol : the ambassador would not
succumb to the prime minister ; neither would the comptroller
to the old eunuch. It is worthy of remark that even the trick
of starving his excellency into compliance is also played off

upon our author at his enviable residence. " The only visible
result upon us, at Yuen-min-yuen, was the abridgment of our
table in the number and quality of our dishes, the usual mode
among the Chinese of manifesting their displeasure." But
these are not the only instances of aping his superiors.
When Lord McCartney rejected his first apartments, at
Hung-ya-yuen, as altogether unfit for his retinue, he was
removed to more spacious lodgings at a palace in Pekin, and
which belonged to the hoopo of Canton. This circumstance,
also, is seized on for a parody. " At Yuen-min-yuen," says
our hero, " after rejecting a set of mean apartments, and very
dirty withal, I succeeded in obtaining some that were larger
and more decent, which, our attendant mandarin took care to
tell me, belonged to one of the ministers of state." (p. 76.)
Now, it is singular that Dr. Dinwiddie, who was equally
interested in all these matters, takes no notice, whatever, of the
threatened bamboo, the abridged table, or the change of
lodgings. The parodies are too palpable to be mistaken, and
others could be produced, all embodying a feeling which, in a
great measure, reveals the true character of the future baronet,
and the secret of his success.

DISMISSAL OF THE EMBASSY.

Returning to the object more immediately under consideration,
we find the comptroller still impressing on his readers that he
is residing at the palace, where he becomes even more bold as
the pretended hour of his removal approaches. After delivering
up all the valuable presents, which he was "not a little delighted
to do," he adds "I gave notice to our small party to be ready
on the following morning to depart for Pekin," (p. 88.) as if
he was not already there, shut up in the ambassador's hotel.
It requires no ordinary amount of patience to put up with such
trashy inventions, but, as we have undertaken to humour him,
he must be allowed to tell his own tale. Two hours after his
arrival in the capital the ambassador and train started on the

homeward journey, leaving our cavalier, and one of his colleagues, behind, to settle accounts at the hotel, as if they had been living at their own expense, or had any accounts to settle. Having settled these accounts, we read: "Mr Maxwell and I, in the evening of the 7th Oct. rode through the streets of Pekin for the last time. We were quite alone, not a single Chinese servant, soldier, nor officer to conduct us; but I had no difficulty in finding the way to and from our hotel to the broad streets, and along which we now proceeded without the least molestation, or indeed I may say without notice." After informing us that the gates are shut at 8, he adds, "We had not much time to spare to save us from being locked within the city walls, and it was at a late hour that we joined the rest of the party in the suburbs of Tong-choo." (p. 89.)

The paragraph, from which the above extracts are taken, is substantially copied from the *Travels*, with, however, one significant attempt at improvement, as shown in the case of the eunuch and the bamboo. The *Travels* does not say for what purpose the comptroller was left in Pekin, after the departure of the embassy, only he was there—mysterious as usual. However, some forty years subsequent to the publication of that "valuable work," this naturally occurred to its author to be an omission, and, in his usual happy humour, he has supplied it by the unaccountable purpose of settling accounts where no accounts existed. From first to last, the expenses of the embassy were defrayed by the emperor; even the smallest article was not allowed to be paid for by the English; nor were the officers and servants suffered to accept of gratuities. In Mr. Barrow's own words: "Under the generous idea of being the emperor's guests, we were not allowed to purchase anything. He alone was to supply our wants, but the officers took the liberty of judging what those wants should consist in." (p. 394.) Where were there any accounts to settle? and what a deplorable excuse for being in Pekin, after the embassy had left! Nor was this all: the restraint put upon their liberties was equally stringent. In short, the gentlemen of the embassy were in a state of little better than actual captivity during their whole stay in China, but particularly so at the capital. "Here," observes Anderson, "we continued to be guarded with the same suspicious vigilance as in our late residence. On no pretence whatever was any one permitted to pass the gates, and every accessible part of the place was under the active care of military power." All this is confirmed to the very letter by Dr. Dinwiddie, who informs us a tent of soldiers constantly guarded the palace, from which there was no egress, but to be again immured in the hotel at Pekin. If the comptroller had a small covered cart always at his disposal it was not to move about, but only as a go-between on this journey of some seven or eight miles; and even then he was no less a prisoner, being constantly under the eye of the official conductor, who was ready to check every step venturing on forbidden ground.(c) Sir George Staunton labors hard to smooth down the asperities of this treatment, but he could not altogether do so. Nor was Mr. Barrow, himself, insensible to this extreme jealousy and watchfulness when he penned the following paragraph : "The morning being very cold, we were desirous to get home as fast as we could; and accordingly galloped along with some of the Tartar cavalry. When we arrived under the walls of Pekin, we turned our horses towards a different gate to that through which we were accustomed to pass, in order to see a little more of the city.(d) But one of our conductors, who had thought it his duty not to lose sight of us, in perceiving us making a wrong turn, hollowed out with all his might. We pushed forward, however, and got through the gate, but we were pursued with such a hue and cry, that we were glad to escape through one of the cross streets leading to our hotel, where we arrived with at least a hundred soldiers at our heels." (p. 120.) At the palace, too, he observes : "If I attempted to move ever so little beyond the court of our apartments, I was sure of being watched and pursued by some of them : to persist in my walk would have thrown the whole palace into an uproar." (p. 233.)

Surrounded by such restraints, this remarkable man, nevertheless, enjoys a freedom of motion that is perfectly staggering. At the palace, he is so watched that he cannot move beyond the court of his apartments; yet he travels a great deal over the forbidden gardens of Yuen-min-yuen. Between that palace and Pekin, he is frequently suffered to go alone; yet he always travelled by the same gate, though anxious to see a little more of the city. When making the attempt to enter by another gate, he is pursued by a troop of soldiers; and yet he is allowed to ride all over the capital, unmolested and unnoticed. To make comments, or to seem surprised at such incompatible movements, is evidently foreign from the purpose of Mr. Barrow, although any honest man, with a reasonable share of common sense, would be trampling on nettles till he had done so. Having laid claim to a greater share of liberty than is usually permitted to strangers in the country, our author has, evidently, applied it to the purpose of creating surprise, by his unaccountable movements, which is left to the reader to unravel, or rather, like the child at the peep show, to take his choice.

The extract relating to the soldiers at his heels, although an evident fabrication, proves to be of considerable use. It not only confirms, up to that late period, how little he had seen of the Chinese capital; but also that he had been accustomed to pass through one gate only, showing, plainly, he was not alone, nor at liberty to travel as he pleased. It also falsifies the assertion, in the *Auto*, which fixes the palace as his place of residence from first to last. He here admits his home was the ambassador's lodgings, in Pekin, which he was so glad to reach from the hue and cry of his pursuers.

With regard to his farewell excursion upon the streets of Pekin, it would, in compiling the *Travels*, naturally appear a desideratum not to show some personal acquaintance with a famous city where he had resided several weeks; and the morning's ramble through the streets of London, by Sir R. Curtis, has, evidently, originated a hint whereon to engraft a few general remarks. These remarks, however, are so despicable that the comptroller would have shown greater sense to have kept the adventure to himself, if it could possibly have happened, and turned out so fruitless.

The abrupt dismissal of the embassy was a pill which the minister-plenipotentiary and his comptroller only could swallow; the former—after much sweetening; the latter—apparently in his sleep; for had he never left England he could not have shown greater ignorance of the indescribable confusion into which the whole train was thrown by only one day's positive notice to remove. While pages are written on what never occurred, not a syllable escapes where pages ought to have been written. Anderson, however, to his credit, has rescued the "*scenes*" from oblivion. Dr. Dinwiddie, too, observes— " so imperative was the command, that many things had to be sent off unpacked." "I was up the greater part of the night, and slept none during the short time I was in bed, owing to the disturbance occasioned by preparing the things for packing." In the midst of this bustle, too, we read "Improper saying of Barrow—*King of England!*" We can guess, but cannot confirm, that allusion was made to his Britannic Majesty demanding some satisfaction for this shameful treatment of his embassy; but whatever was the meaning, the entry is significant—the comptroller was at his post, amidst the very bustle and noise over which he has thrown an impenetrable veil. The *Auto*, for sure, would fain persuade us he was in a state of happy ignorance, at Yuen-min-yuen, from whence he arrived only two hours previous to the ambassador's departure from Pekin. *Credat Judaes Appelles!*

*   *   *   *   *   *   *   *   *

Such is a glimpse of the complexion which this enviable residence, at the Chinese capital, is likely to assume before the statements of the witnesses. We admit it is of little interest, and certainly of no consequence, excepting always the confidence to be reposed in the *dicta* of reputed authority.

Our private journal could "a tale unfold," proving, to the satisfaction of every reasonable man, that the entire history of the comptroller, at Yuen-min-yuen, is neither more nor less than the detestable vaporings of unbridled vanity, with scarcely the shadow of a foundation to work upon; but the proof would rest upon a solitary individual showing the most inconceivable ignorance of, or substituting stubborn facts in the place of others blazoned forth in the name of truth. It happens, well, that there is a better mode of testing the validity of our author's statements, and we now proceed to the second part of our engagement, the Investigation of the origin of those incidents and other occurrences, so profusely scattered throughout the body of the mis-named " Travels in China." That it is a *mis-nomer* we expect to satisfy the most scrupulous inquirer, if only possessed of common honesty.

INVESTIGATION

OF THE

"FACTS AND OBSERVATIONS"

OF THE

"TRAVELS IN CHINA,"

OTHERWISE THE

"LARGE QUARTO"

SENTIMENTS ON THE FACTS AND OBSERVATIONS.

SPEAKING of the sentiments advanced in these *Travels*, our author, in his advertisement, declares "they are the unbiassed conclusions of his own mind, founded altogether on his own observations."

When about to commence the narrative, he also declares, "The opinions they contain are drawn from such incidents and anecdotes as occurred in the course of an eight months' visit, and from such as seemed best calculated to illustrate the condition of the people, the national character, and the nature of the government. A short residence in the imperial palace of Yuen-min-yuen, a greater share of liberty than is usually permitted to strangers in this country, with the assistance of some little knowledge of the language, afforded me the means of collecting the facts and observations which I now lay before the public." (p. 31.)

Having commenced the narrative, our author once more declares—" Had we returned to Europe, without proceeding farther in the country than *Tiensing*, a most lively impression would always have remained on my mind in favor of the Chinese. But a variety of incidents that afterwards occurred, and a more intimate acquaintance with their manners and habits, produced a woeful change of sentiment in this respect. Of such incidents, as may tend.to illustrate the moral character of this extraordinary people, I shall relate a few that were the most striking, in taking a general view of their state of society, to which, and to the nature of the executive government, all their moral actions may be referred." (p. 82.)

Respecting the incidents here alluded to, or by whatever name the " facts and observations" are known, we intend to show that, instead of the character being deduced from the incident, the case is *exactly the reverse* : the incident is deduced from the character. The explanation will be more complete by observing—the incidents, and other occurrences, brought forward as illustrations, are, themselves, concocted for the sole purpose of bolstering up prejudices, and preconceived notions about China and the Chinese. And we further believe, numerous though they be, every incident, " fact, or observation," without exception, is more or less subject to this rule. The first instance we shall adduce is the

ECLIPSE AT TONCHOO.

" A rude projection of a lunar eclipse, that happened whilst we were at *Tongchoo*, was stuck up in the corners of the streets ; all the officers were in mourning, and all business was suspended for that day." (p. 287.)

A circumstance exercising such an influence on the embassy could not have been overlooked by the two chiefs ; in verity, we deny the possibility of their doing so : nowhere, however, is this day of *rest and mourning* alluded to, either at Tonchoo,

or any other place. On the contrary, every account confirms
that both the government officials, and the gentlemen of the
embassy, continued, all the time, unceasing with their prepara-
tions for the journey.(e) It is, nevertheless, true that the
projection of an eclipse was seen in the streets, but it was
only "to happen soon afterwards;" and, unfortunately for
Mr. Barrow's "observations," *did not happen* while the embassy
remained at Tonchoo. Instead thereof, it was at Hun-ya-yuen,
some seven miles on the other side of Pekin. In short, the
eclipse occurred late at night, commencing at a quarter-past
nine, August 21,(f) the most bustling day of all others, when
the embassy passed through the capital; and when the officers
were neither in mourning, nor was business suspended.

Dr. Dinwiddie, perhaps the only individual of the embassy
who took an active interest in the matter, had calculated and
projected the eclipse, during the passage up the Pyho. At
Tonchoo, he presented Lord McCartney with a type and all
particulars; and at Hung-ya-yuen, anxious to know the result
of his calculations, he watched the progress of the event, when
every other person of the train was either locked in the embrace
of Morpheus, or resting from the fatigues of the day.

To the origin of this incident, or occurrence, then, our
author, grasping at every suitable bit of information on China,
reads in the accounts of the Dutch embassy of a solar and also
a lunar eclipse, and the influence which these events exercised
on that mission. This was something worth knowing, and,
accordingly, the eager gentleman draws a parallel to show
that it was nothing new to him; but, unhappily, he has
shown what never happened. He has brought forward a
certain event, and a certain consequence of that event; but
as the event did not take place, the consequence did not
follow; confirming, what the history of the mission proves,
there was no day of mourning and rest at Tonchoo.

This is the first specimen selected from the "facts and
observations" upon which the "unbiassed conclusions have
been founded," and we fancy our readers will agree with

us, they are founded with a vengeance. The "motive" is evidently worthy of its attribute — it is "powerful." Fortunately, for the cause of truth, the occurrence is one that does not depend upon an eye-witness; it is open to all men, and all times, and demands a careful consideration, furnishing, as it does, the key to unlock the history of every incident, anecdote, or occurrence brought forward as illustrations in the "Travels in China." A piece of acceptable information is picked up from reading or conversation, or it may be the result of prejudice, or an unintelligible whim; but from whatever source, an incident of some kind or other is invented, by which it may appear as an "observation" of our author himself. To give it weight, some colorable pretext is usually fixed upon, as in the case of this eclipse, which was "to happen soon afterwards." Upon such facts, and such *only*, have the "Travels in China" been reared.

It will be well to notice how little Mr. Barrow has to say about this day of mourning and rest at Tonchoo. He knew he was treading on ground too dangerous to enter into particulars, and consequently we have not a syllable beyond that it happened, as stated in the extract: even the very day is kept out of sight. He has, however, besides pointing out the days, many particulars to tell us respecting the two occasions mentioned by the Dutch, showing, conclusively, that he relied upon their experience to supply the information which should have been furnished by his own.

But we shall now prove from Mr. Barrow, himself, the imposition he has practised on mankind, yes! in the face of the honorary initials united to his name. Unable, with all his cunning, to bury it in oblivion, the eventful day oozes out, and it happens to be the most unfortunate one that could have been selected for his purpose. Had the eclipse occurred a day earlier, or a day later, a doubt might possibly have remained in the minds of some, but cannot now, as will be shown from the *Travels*, which, of their own accord, scatter to the winds the devotional purposes of the 21st August.

" According to the arrangement, on the 21st of August,
about three o'clock in the morning, we were prepared to set
out, but could scarcely be said to be fairly in motion till five,
and before we had cleared the city of *Tongchoo*, it was past
six o'clock. From this city to the capital, I may venture to
say, the road never before exhibited so motley a group. In
front marched about three thousand porters, carrying six
hundred packages; some of which were so large and heavy,
as to require thirty-two bearers: with these were mixed a
proportionate number of inferior officers, each having the
charge and superintendence of a division. Next followed
eighty-five waggons, and thirty-nine hand-carts, each with
one wheel, loaded with wine, porter, and other European
provisions, ammunitions, and such heavy articles as were not
liable to be broken. Eight light field pieces, which were
among the presents for the emperor, closed this part of the
procession. After these paraded the Tartar legate, and
several officers from court, with their numerous attendants;
some on horseback, some in chairs, and others on foot. Then
followed the ambassador's guards in waggons, the servants,
musicians, and mechanics, also in waggons; the gentlemen of
the suite on horseback, the ambassador, the minister plenipotentiary, his son, and the interpreter, in four ornamented
chairs; the rest of the suite in small covered carriages on
two wheels, not unlike in appearance to our funeral hearses,
but only half the length; and last of all Van and Chou, with
their attendants, closed this motley procession."(*g*) (p. 88.)

Let the reader now turn to the extract at page 48; let him
look on this picture, and then on that, and mark the extraordinary purposes to which the same day is devoted by the same
author. Let him fancy he sees the Chinese officers robed in
their mourning habiliments, and withdrawn from all business
to their private devotions, leaving the embassy itself to peace
and quietness, in the temple of Tonchoo. Let him again revert
to the bustling cavalcade, and the exciting scenes on the road
to Pekin; let him gaze on the two pictures, if he can, without

amazement, and ask himself if accident, or any kind of oversight, exercised the remotest influence in producing this contrast.   Let him ask again if the devotional ceremonies of the
Chinese officers are not rather the result of a deep laid scheme.
But lest some mode of explanation might possibly yet remain ;
lest some redeeming quality might possibly yet apologise for a
solitary breach of faith, let him withhold that answer till he
has followed us to the end of this inquiry.

Before quitting this example, we have yet another observation
to make.   It will be found that Mr. Barrow not unfrequently
produces these parallels, *i.e.* corroborating his own experience
by the experience of others ; but our eyes once opened, we
scan with suspicion what otherwise might have passed unnoticed.
On a close inspection, the peculiarities of the eclipse is, more
or less, detected in other cases ; and, at all events, this outrageous plagiarism is *primâ facie* evidence of the worthlessness
of such corroborations.

SCORPIONS AT TONCHOO.

Our next illustration is also at Tonchoo, where the
embassy was lodged in a temple, " among the gods of the
nation."   From Sir George Staunton, we learn—" In some of
the rooms the priests had suffered scorpions and scolopendras
to harbour through neglect."   On this hint, the comptroller
enlarges in the following manner : " The room, in which
some of us *should* have slept, was so full of scorpions and
scolopendras, and these animals crept in such numbers into
our beds, that we were fairly driven out, and obliged to swing
our cots in the open air, between two trees."   (p. 487.)

This circumstance is calculated to arouse attention in the
most insensate of individuals, and particularly in those who
had never experienced the like ; yet, strange enough, both
Lord McCartney and Anderson are unconscious that " these
animals" were creeping about the temple at all.   Surely, in

such a nursery, they could not all be confined to one room ; still these journalists are as silent on their second, as on their first arrival. Dr. Dinwiddie, however, takes notice of a solitary scorpion being seen the first night they lodged in the temple, and, as he happened to be one of the gentlemen in the room so frightfully infested, we give his evidence entire. " After a day of great fatigue, we returned to the temple to supper, and went to bed at eight o'clock. Eight gentlemen were to have slept in one apartment, but Captain McIntosh and Mr. Maxwell preferred the portico ; and, in consequence of the scorpion, Dr. Gillan followed." Thus, the frightful phantom, conjured up by the " large quarto," all but vanishes, throwing completely into shade the story of the *three black crows*.

From this incident our author deduces the want of cleanliness in the persons and apartments of the priests, in *all* the principal temples. How was he to know that this temple was a type of all the others ? the information could not be derived from his own " facts and observations ; " it could only be second hand, at best. Apparently through prejudice, but from whatever cause, the "*unbiassed*" gentleman has come to the conclusion that the priests, in all the principal temples of China, are a dirty set of men ; and this is proved by " such numbers " of scorpions at Tonchoo, nowhere else. But we have shown that even the solitary incident, at Tonchoo, with all the importance given to it by Sir George Staunton, is an outrageous exaggeration, all but a fiction. A most insignificant occurrence is purposely magnified to blacken the character of the priests, previously decided on. The principle is exactly the same as in the last example ; a single scorpion appeared and gave the color for the incident.

The reader has already had evidence, and will have more, that much dependance is not always to be placed in the elegant and accurate details of the official account, the author of which was not a lodger in the vicious room. It will be seen, too, that the *we* this and the *we* that of the comptroller carries no definite or intelligible meaning. Of three gentlemen who left the room, only one was driven out; the other two having, previously, preferred the open portico, to the close air of the chamber. Mr. Barrow was not even one of the three; it is doubtful if he even saw the " animal."

In the two illustrations, now adduced, a single allusion to the subject only is made, in each case; but whenever an incident comes twice under the notice of our author, he seldom, if ever, fails to commit himself, and the following is a most flagrant proof.

" CANTON ULCER."

" On arriving at the northern extremity of the province of Canton, one of our conductors had imprudently passed the night in one of those houses where, by the license of govern- ment, females are allowed to prostitute their persons in order to gain a livelihood. Here, it seems, he had caught the infection, and after suffering a considerable degree of pain, and no less alarm, he communicated to our physician the symptoms of his complaint, of the nature and cause of which he was entirely ignorant." (p. 352.)

Turning to the narrative, we find Nanyang (h) the first station in the province of Canton where the embassy passed the night. We also find, upon the morning following their arrival—" The officers, assembled here from different parts of the country, detained us a whole day in order to have an opportunity of laying their several complaints before our physician, at the recommendation of Vantagin, who had felt the good effects of his practice." (p. 593.)

So it appears that Vantagin, the conductor alluded to in the first extract, must have caught the infection, the disease must have ripened, and it must have been cured, all in the space of one night! Nay, the cure must have been instant- aneous on the following morning; and as the officers were on the spot, ready with their diseases, how else but on lightning

wings could the news have sped to the different parts of the
country! Perfect as we consider our system of railway and
telegraphic communication, it would seem but a mere mock
in comparison of the appliances of China, at the period in
question. That Van should have recommended the practice
of such a physician is no wonder; but how was he, novice as
he was, to know and take such an interest in his fellow officers,
scattered abroad in the province, and to whom he must have been
a total stranger? But this is not all: instead of being detained
here "a whole day," for this truly patriotic purpose, we have
the most conclusive evidence that the barges sailed that *very
morning*, so soon as the baggage was got aboard. (*i*) Even
this is confirmed by Mr. Barrow, himself, in a "carefully
constructed" map, (accompanying the official account,) which
shows upon that very day the embassy, instead of being at a
stand still, made its usual progress.

In Canton, where time and other circumstances rendered
the matter a probability, Sir George Staunton mentions some
mandarins deriving such a benefit from the physician. This,
no doubt, originated the illucidating incident of the truly
observant Mr. Barrow, who, to be first in the field with his
information, has transferred the particulars to the northern
extremity of the province. In doing so, he has trumped up
a most disgusting impossibility, for what he ostensibly calls
"an instance of usurped superiority condescending to ask advice
of barbarians;" but which, in reality, is to show his own
knowledge of the influences which the contact with Europeans
have exercised on this part of the empire.

Here, again, the same principle is at work to produce
a piece of information which, in this instance, is picked out of
the official volumes. Turning the author of his good fortune
to every possible advantage, these volumes have been carefully
overhauled for suitable subjects to be repeated in the *Travels*;
and as a general rule, the particulars of the information have
been removed to another locality, and so as to happen under
different circumstances. A new occurrence is thus contrived

and blazoned forth among the "facts and observations," which have been hazarded with a degree of boldness challenging competition.

If the features attending the eclipse, at Tonchoo, might reasonably have escaped the attention of the critics, we think the incident of the "Canton ulcer" ought to have drawn their attention. They had not to travel from the volume where a manifest impossibility was staring them in the face. Instead of pointing out such disgusting trumpery, in forcible terms, the author of it is congratulated on his "good sense," and his faithful record. All this, however, only proves how superficially the *Travels* have been read, and the little dependence that can be placed on reviews, in general. Mr. Barrow, himself, as a reviewer, makes a merit of his connexion with the *Quarterly*, the editor of which thought the man who could write the Embassy to China was a fit and proper person to review the works of other men. The few specimens we have produced, from that embassy, are not very creditable to the acumen of the great critic; they show either his ignorance of the atmosphere in which he moved, or that he sought the assistance of Mr. Barrow on the principle of *set a rogue*.

"FOREIGN DEVILS."

Nanyang is also the scene of another adventure, which, though not improbable in itself, is perfectly worthless for the purpose it is told.

"Hitherto the embassy had met with the greatest respect and civility from all classes of the natives, but now even the peasantry ran out of their houses, as we passed, and bawled after us opprobrious and contemptuous expressions, signifying *foreign devils*." " The further we advanced the more rude and insolent they became." (p. 591.)

To this it may be replied that, unless two abrupt suspicious lines in Lord McCartney's journal, no other person takes the least notice of such insolence, which they must have done, if it increased in proportion as the embassy advanced. Of this the insulted gentleman, himself, gives no further proof than the instance just quoted, and yet we are forced to the conclusion that, by the time he reached Canton, the insolence of the Chinese would have acquired an impetus that would have forced him to some further comments upon it.

But is it true that they had, previously to their arrival at Nanyang, met with the greatest respect and civility from all classes of the natives ? Did the crowd at Tinghai show the greatest respect and civility in stopping his palanquin *every moment*, that every one might thrust in his head at the window, exclaiming with a grin, "*Hungmau, Redpate ?*" Did the soldier, who interrupted the gentlemen in their walks, and whose ears were bored for his "*insolence*," behave with the greatest respect and civility ? Did his commanding officer, who was bambooed and stripped of his authority for the same offence, behave with the greatest respect and civility ? Did the men of Kanchoo, who furnished the *rootless* varnish plants, play a *trick upon strangers* in the true spirit of the nation ? Did the prime minister, the Tartar legate, and the ex-viceroy of Canton show any *hauteur and want of complaisance* ? In short : was the *suspicious and watchful* conduct of the government to strangers suited to the free and independent spirit of Britons ? Let the man who had hitherto "met with the greatest respect and civility, from all classes of the natives," answer ; and he does so, in every instance, against himself.

A single circumstance will often decide a question which a thousand testimonies would only tend to confirm ; and, again, fortunately for the cause of truth, our author, himself, furnishes that circumstance. "It is due to the inhabitants to declare that I never met with the slightest insult, nor interruption from any class of the Chinese population, whether official or plebian ; but on the contrary, the most civil and courteous conduct, from the highest to the lowest, with a willing dispo. sition always to oblige." (p. 115.)

Language could not furnish a flatter denial than the last quotation does to the first, respecting the "foreign devils," as well as to the various insults, tricks and interruptions, asserted to have been met with on the embassy, and which are turned to good advantage, when necessary, in elucidating Chinese character.   But to the origin of this outburst of popular contempt : there is good reason to believe that most of the general information picked up by the embassy occurred at the journey's end, where the only opportunities presented themselves.   The influences resulting from the contact with foreigners, as annunciated in the "Canton ulcer," and the "foreign devils," were undoubtedly acquired here, if acquired in China ; the comptroller, however, in hot haste to point out his knowledge of these influences, has thrust them forward, in their most aggravated forms, at the very threshold of the province.   In our opinion, this is not very consistent with "good sense ; " particularly since we have shown the one to be an impossibility, and the other valueless.   They are thus proved from our author, himself, and consequently occurrences contrived for their respective purposes.

WANT OF FELLOW-FEELING.—Accident at Linsin.

The mode by which the reader of the *Travels* is made acquainted with the illucidating incidents has something remarkable about it : they are introduced almost universally in a solitary state, each for its particular object ; a small proportion only being noticed in the course of the narrative.   In this peculiar way, abstracted from their connecting links in the embassy, the greatest scope is presented for the exercise of predilections, while it becomes a very difficult matter for a reader to detect discrepancies, which would be seen at a glance if attempted to be joined to the regular chain of occurrences. A striking illustration of this is furnished in an accident on the homeward journey.   Introduced in this disguise, we read :

"In the course of our journey down the grand canal we had occasion to witness a scene, which was considered as a remarkable example of a want of fellow-feeling. Of the number of persons who had crowded down to the banks of the canal several had posted themselves upon the high projecting stern of an old vessel which, unfortunately, breaking down with the weight, the whole group tumbled with the wreck into the canal, just at the moment when the yachts of the embassy were passing. Although numbers of boats were sailing about the place, none were perceived to go to the assistance of those that were struggling in the water. They even seemed not to know that such an accident had happened, nor could the shrieks of the boys, floating on pieces of the wreck, attract their attention. One fellow was observed very busily employed in picking up, with his boathook, the hat of a drowning man. It was in vain we endeavored to prevail on the people of our vessel to heave-to and send the boat to their assistance. It is true, we were then going at the rate of seven miles an hour, which was the plea they made for not stopping. I have no doubt that several of these unfortunaate people must inevitably have perished." (p. 166.)

Any person reading the foregoing paragraph would naturally conclude that the embassy had been some days, at least, in the canal, and was dashing along, in broad day-light, with the wind and current in their favor. From Sir George Staunton, however, we find the fleet entered the canal at Linsin, not far from which the accident happened ; and from Lord McCartney, that they passed Linsin at 4 P.M., and before dark got into a narrow canal. Here, then, from the talents just mentioned, it is evident the accident—if occurring in the canal—must have been immediately on their entrance, because it was near Linsin, and while there was yet light, circumstances which never afterwards occurred in conjunction. A numerous fleet, then, entering a narrow canal, with a strong opposing current, and the shades of even descending, does not appear quite consistent with the description, and with so rapid a rate as *affirmed*.

But, to all this, we have the most satisfactory testimony, from our manuscript authority, that the fleet—on entering the canal—came to rest, which was the only stopping of the yachts before Linsin. We have, moreover, the same satisfactory testimony that the accident occurred *in the river*, some five or six miles back; even the very hour of the day is specified.

But whether in the river, or in the canal, the yachts were contending with a current of some three miles an hour. It commenced at Tiensing, on entering the Euho river, and did not cease till reaching the summit level of the canal, four days after passing Linsin. All along, too, the breeze was more or less baffling, *never* propitious; while the trackers, eighteen to twenty to each vessel, to use Barrow's formula, "were fitter for an hospital than performing any kind of labor." In short, the united testimony of Lord McCartney, Sir George Staunton, Dr. Dinwiddie, and even of our author himself, confirm how slow their progress was all along this stage of the journey; that it seldom, or never, exceeded two miles an hour, instead of seven, and consequently the Chinese boatmen *never* made use of such a "plea" to avoid going to the rescue. At the very moment of the accident, the rate, singularly enough, is indisputably fixed under two miles an hour.

This is one of the very few real incidents occurring on the embassy, and the simple narrative of it, by Dr. Dinwiddie, is sufficiently affecting, without any attempt at extraneous coloring. "At two, just as we were sitting down to dinner, part of the stern of a junk, lying in the river, yielded to the weight of spectators, when a number were thrown into the river, and some in great danger. The spectators seemed but little affected by the accident." Now this observation implies a termination of the accident, although our *unbiassed* author struggles to persuade his readers that some of the unfortunate people perished. A single minute, however, at the *dashing rate*, would have put it out of his power to have formed any idea as to the ultimate result, even in day light, and much less if evening had set in, which must have been the case had the accident happened in the canal. The real circumstances attending this casualty are so distorted that the casualty itself is all but invented; and it is quite clear the gentleman in search of facts has been spurred on to make the most of it, not to be outdone by another instance of indifference to human suffering, recorded in the Dutch embassy. The history of that mission will be found to have supplied many of the subsequent views, or "woful change," he now struggles to maintain.

Connected with this event is another flagrant fallacy. The embassy passed the pagoda of Linsin at one o'clock; the accident occurred at two, just within the north wall of the city; and between these points, distant from one to two miles, the barges *never* stopped, nor even that day, until they rested within the first floodgate of the canal. If Mr. Barrow, therefore, had been ashore, at the pagoda, as insinuated in the narrative, (p. 503) he could not have seen the accident from his barge; but the probability is he was aboard, and that the visit to the pagoda is only another instance of squeezing in a whim, or bit of information, so as to appear emanating from himself. In this *his forte lay*. We shall yet have occasion to speak of the pagoda of Linsin.

To establish the position adverted to at the commencement of the example, we add the following observation: In its abstracted view, the incident exhibits nothing improbable in its proportions, unless the rapid rate might induce a momentary suspicion, otherwise it could not but pass current; but when its place is sought for, in the embassy, how clumsy every circumstance appears. In the first place: the accident did not occur in the canal, but in the river, nearly opposite the north wall of the city of Linsin, where the current, instead of favoring a seven miles rate, was so strong against them that their real progress was under two miles. Again: our ubiquitous author is not only aboard at the time of the accident, but also ashore at the pagoda, less than two miles distant, and between which places the vessels never stopped. The stubborn

E

fact of the accident occurring in the river, with the exact locality and the hour of the day, pointed out, exhibit, in all their deformity, the detestable details of the comptroller, and particularly the disgraceful " plea" put into the mouths of the Chinese boatmen.

INHUMANITY.—First Illustration.

The "want of fellow-feeling," like nearly every subject, is dismissed by a single instance ; but the next one, however, " inhumanity," is fertile of incidents, and a deal of capital is forced out of it, evidently to counteract the statements of Anderson, who has recorded the particulars of an English soldier, at Gehol, undergoing the lash to the disgust of the Chinese spectators.   In support of his predilections, our author relates an incident in such a manner as to make the "Authentic Account" of Sir George Staunton unworthy of the name, and perfectly meagre.

" One day an officer of high rank took it into his head to interrupt the gentlemen in their usual walk, and for this purpose dispatched after them nine or ten of his soldiers, who forced them in a rude manner to return to the vessels.   Our two conductors *Van* and *Chou*, being made acquainted with the circumstance, gave to each of the soldiers a most severe flogging.   One of these, who had been particularly insolent, had his ears bored through with iron wire, and his hands bound to them for several days.   The viceroy of Canton was at this time with the embassy, and being in rank superior to the offending officer, he ordered the latter to appear before him, gave him a severe reprimand, and sentenced him to receive forty strokes of the bamboo as a *gentle correction*.   Our two Chinese friends were particularly pressing that the gentlemen insulted should be present at the punishment of the officer, and it was not without difficulty they could be persuaded that such a scene would not afford them any gratification." (p. 163.)

On the same occasion, Sir George Staunton observes, "Choutazin and Vantazin had the soldiers laid flat on the floor and held by some of the military attendants, while others were ordered to strike them with a piece of slit bamboo ; but the persons who were ill-treated succeeded in obtaining for the soldiers a remission of that sentence." (II. p. 488.)

Can both accounts be true ? or rather is not an imposition stamped upon the very face of the statements ? No sane man will think a "remission of the sentence" compatible with a "most severe flogging." But how could Sir George Staunton ignore the most extraordinary part of the punishment, the boring of the soldier's ears, to which his hands were tied, for several days, with iron wire ? Was he not in possession of Mr Barrow's journal and all his "loose notes?" If the chief co-adjutor to the great compilation has not hood-winked his patron, by systematically keeping back the most wonderful of these "notes," we are forced to the alternative, which is likely, that the information about *ear-boring* was a subsequent discovery, and, no doubt, thinking it a valuable addition to the incident, he has dove-tailed it in, regardless of the perspective in which it places the "Authentic Account." An argument with Mr. Barrow, evidently, possesses force in proportion to its extravagance, and he has, here, proved himself a match for the "livery servant;" still, we are lost in amazement that he should thus triumph at the expense of his benefactor.

Of the numerous contradictions, indirectly it is true, heaped, by the publication of the *Travels*, upon the official volumes, the reviewers, mentioned in this work, have never fallen on a single instance ; and this is the more remarkable as Mr. Barrow, having pledged himself for the accuracy of these volumes, is answerable for both accounts. The case on hand was surely one to have called for some comments, carrying as it does the stamp of an imposition in its very face. To allow an author of "growing reputation," thus, to trifle with public sentiment seems strange indeed. A certain occurrence we are assured has been "detailed with equal elegance and accuracy ;" never-

theless, the assurer produces another set of details, totally at
variance with the former, and, without assigning any reason,
bids the public swallow both.   If this is not humbug the world
may be safely challenged to produce an instance.   The imposition is too bare-faced ; and how has it been allowed with
impunity ?   An implicit reliance on the *dicta* of authority often
serves to confirm and propagate a belief in the grossest errors.
Every anecdote, or occurrence of any interest, related by
Sir George Staunton, has re-appeared in the *Travels;* and it
is a remarkable fact that they are always in a more *humourous*
or more *marvellous* dress—in some instances to such an extent
as to render the original worthless.   The present is an example,
and beyond doubt a pure invention from its very foundation.(*j*)
But even admitting the most trifling consideration could be
raked up for the incident, even that would not acquit it of
imposition, and nobody seems to be aware of such trashy
inventions staining the records of an important national event.
On the contrary, the two historians have been flattered as
" able writers," and the improved version as a " valuable
addition " to the " splendid account " previously detailed.

INHUMANITY.—Second Illustration.

Also on Chinese inhumanity, a subject our author is bent on
upholding, at whatever cost, we read :
" Whenever it was found necessary to track the vessels
against the stream, a number of men were always pressed into
this disagreeable and laborious service, for which they were to
receive about sixpence a day so long as they tracked, without
any allowance being made to them for returning to the place
from whence they were forced.   These people knowing the
difficulty there was of getting others to supply their places, and
that their services would be required until such should be procured, generally deserted by night, disregarding their pay.   In
order to procure others, the officers dispatched their soldiers to

the nearest village, taking the inhabitants by surprise, and forcing them out of their beds to join the yachts. Scarcely a night occurred in which some poor wretches did not suffer the lashes of the soldiers for attempting to escape, or for pleading the excuse of old age, or infirmity. It was painful to behold the deplorable condition of some of these creatures. Several were half naked, and appeared to be wasting and languishing for want of food. Yet the task of dragging along the vessels was far from being light. Sometimes they were under the necessity of wading to the middle in mud; sometimes to swim across creeks, and immediately afterwards to expose their naked bodies to a scorching sun; and they were always driven by a soldier or the lictor of some petty police officer carrying in his hand an enormous whip, with which he lashed them with as little reluctance as if they had been a team of horses." (p. 161.)

After this, Anderson might as well give in : however, it is vain that we search the records of all the other witnesses for a confirmation of this unprecedented string of brutalities. On the first arrival of the embassy, even then, it was found necessary to track the vessels up the Pyho, where the tracksmen were sometimes wading to the middle in mud; sometimes swimming across creeks, and immediately afterwards exposing their naked bodies to a scorching sun. All this is susceptible of the strongest proof; but it was only on this occasion—not afterwards. An August sun and a constant cloudless sky were overhead; but on their return these features were very different, and the people, instead of being half naked, everywhere had assumed their winter habits. So far, however, from wasting and languishing for want of food, all accounts mention the trackers on the Pyho in the most praiseworthy terms, not only for ability, but also for cheerfulness and willingness. Our private record sums up thus : " In perpetually tracking against the current of a strong stream, without the least aid from the wind, the men were sometimes up to the middle in water and mud ; at other times obliged to swim across rivulets, entering

the Pyho—all this with great cheerfulness—no murmuring.
Nor does it seem to proceed so much from the commands of
the mandarine as from a natural willingness to do their duty.
The men who transhipped our luggage, under a most exces-
sively hot sun, neither asked money nor drink, though they do
not dislike samsu—even get tipsy with it.   Their dexterity,
in hoisting up, and, still more, in carrying the heaviest boxes,
appeared to me superior to any thing I had seen in Europe."
Sir George Staunton, too, repeating the observations of Lord
McCartney, says, " They were well made, muscular men, but
remarkably round shouldered ; " and Mr. Barrow, whose narrative endorses the very sentiments of Dr. Dinwiddie, admits
" the same cheerful and willing mind had constantly shown
itself on all occasions, by all those who were employed in the
service of the embassy."   (p. 80.)   Again : " Everything
here, in fact, seems to be at the instant command of the state ;
and the most laborious tasks are undertaken and executed with
a readiness, and even a chearfulness, which one could scarcely
expect to meet with in so despotic a government."   (p. 88.)

The men, then, were not only *able* and *willing* to do their
duty, but *did* do it, with a cheerfulness remarkable even to
that authority which affirms they were *always* pressed into the
disagreeable service, and lashed, by the lictor of a petty police
officer, as if they had been a team of horses.   Where could
the lictor find excuse for such a wanton abuse of authority ?
and how is it that the colleagues of our author, evidently more
interested than himself in this laborious dragging, never once
detects the lashes of this " enormous whip," though always at
its hellish work.   Strange enough, on other occasions, from
our author too, we learn that the soldiers, though active and
noisy in brandishing their whips, never let them fall upon the
people.

A careful review of all the circumstances exposes a mad
determination to uphold his detestable whims on inhumanity,
with the merits of which, as a question, we have nothing to do ;
our sole object being to expose the baseless foundations upon

which the comptroller has built his whims. A one-sided view of a case, however correctly detailed, is evidence of dishonesty, and it is still more so if invention, or exaggeration, is resorted to to carry conviction. How significantly is every circumstance colored to give effect to this display of inhumanity! The dragging is *laborious* and *disagreeable;* the tracksmen are *wasting* and *languishing* for want of food; always *pressed* into the service, and *lashed* like a team of horses, notwithstanding their deplorable condition of body. Even *age* and *infirmity* afford no protection from the *enormous* whip, whose proprietor is also a *character* the most unlikely to let it remain idle. To crown all, a paltry recompense is the *only reward* of these ill-fated wretches. The argument would have lost nothing had one or two of them expired beneath the load. This, indeed, only was wanting to put the last stroke to a picture already all but perfect, and it may appear curious how a prolific genius overlooked such a self-evident feature, particularly when he had the experience of the Dutch to furnish him with another parallel. It was, however, colored enough to have driven the most sanguine abolitionist to despair, had there not been the means of detecting the imposture, and restoring consolation.(*k*)

If there is one thing more conspicuous than another, in these *Travels*, the statements which, everywhere, start up opposing force to force may justly claim this pre-eminence. It is scarcely possible to point out a whim, or speculation, that is not, more or less, confuted on another page. Any subject indeed, the "facts and observations," themselves, if twice under notice, exposes some contradiction or other; and this arises, in a great measure, from mingling together a mass of information picked up from numerous conflicting sources; but still more from a ready acquiescence to ignore the obligations of truth. The traveller, who gathers interesting "facts and observations" from other travellers, and who stores remarkable sentiments and ideas from other writers, will find it nice work, even with an honest intention, to keep within the pale of consistency; and it requires little penetration to perceive the consequences of filling a " large quarto," solely to produce a flourish.   Whatever conclusions a writer may come to on any subject, whether well investigated or not, even if it is a whim, it behoves him, above all things, to be consistent with himself.

INHUMANITY.—Third Illustration.

We introduce another illustration of the same detestable whim ; one, indeed, that cannot be quite so flatly confuted, but nevertheless involved in mystery, and sufficiently explanatory of the difficulties besetting our author's most unassailable observations.

" In our return down the *Peiho*, the water being considerably shallower than when we first sailed up this river, one of our accommodation barges got aground in the middle of the night. The air was piercing cold, and the poor creatures belonging to the vessel were busy until sunrise, in the midst of the river, using their endeavours to get her off.   The rest of the fleet had proceeded, and the patience of the superintending officer at length being exhausted, he ordered his soldiers to flog the captain and the whole crew ; which was accordingly done in a most unmerciful manner: and this was their only reward for the use of the yacht, their time and labour for two days." (p. 161.)

Here we have a boat stranded, and the boatmen brutally treated for what they could not help.   What sort of a journalist must he be who could overlook such a circumstance ?   Both Sir George Staunton and Dr. Dinwiddie are attentive to the tedious drawbacks in descending the river, yet they ignore this untoward event, *in toto* ; and this is very remarkable in regard to the baronet, who was in possession of all the "loose notes." Lord McCartney, however, is made to observe, " One of the yachts being somewhat larger than the others, and more heavily laden, was not able to proceed, and Mr. Maxwell,

Captain McIntosh, and Dr. Gillan, &c., were obliged to remove into smaller boats, and divide the baggage." This is the only sentiment tending to support the incident. But if his lordship knew the boat stuck fast, surely he knew the unmerited treatment of the men; yet he ignores it. Nay! it is unaccountable he should allow it to stick fast at all, without some comment, as he affirms the men could not only drag, but lift the vessels over such obstacles. "It is quite wonderful to see the strength and expertness of the Chinese boatmen, who, by main bodily might, often dragged and lifted over sands and gravel, almost dry, the yachts we travelled in, some of which were heavy laden, and seventy feet in length by twelve in the beam, and drew not more than ten inches water." Is it likely his lordship would write two such antagonistic statements without some explanation? Though cloaked with his name, the first has every characteristic of another forgery, of which we shall yet have occasion to speak, being satisfied that shameless liberties have been taken with his lordship's journal. At present there is something striking in the mode of introducing the gentlemen by name, while it is curious that the place of Mr. Barrow is supplied by an &c., although on all other occasions this honorable personage is so conspicuously stuck in the front as to be remarkable, even to a child. But there is sufficient evidence, from the comptroller himself, to show that the fleet continued of the same number of vessels from Tonchoo to Hanchoo, and that he had the same fellow-companions throughout this journey, proving the separation, mentioned by Lord McCartney, did not take place. And to this, the united testimony of the witnesses prove the vessels were all alike, of the lightest construction, admitted *very little luggage*, drew only ten inches water, and the dragging, though attended with trouble and delay, was not an impossibility. The Chinese authorities, also, were too wide awake; they knew every difficulty, and how to provide against it. However, beyond the mere fact that one of the boats stuck fast, and could not be got off, we only learn the following traits of inhumanity, and they are bad. The *piercing cold* air ; the *fruitless* endeavors of the *poor* people in the *midst* of the river; and the *most unmerciful* flogging, the *only reward* for two days use of the yacht, time, and labor. But the entry in Lord McCartney's journal proves there were *four* days use of the yacht, time, and labor, which, besides making the case worse for the poor boatmen, makes it even so for the comptroller. Another circumstance, while mitigating the miseries of the ill-used men, only adds to the difficulties of the champion of humanity. The thermometer, in the open air, that morning, at sun rise, was no less than 52°, and the water, being little more than ankle deep, scarcely indicates a degree of " piercing cold," or that the situation of the poor creatures was so very deplorable. From this circumstance, alone, it may fairly be inferred that the " unmerciful flogging" was not so unmerciful after all. We are persuaded, indeed, that the incident is, altogether, one of the most disgraceful fabrications of which an author was ever suspected ; and for no other purpose but upholding an execrable whim, in opposition to the flogging at Gehol. It may be equalled, but not outdone, by any other incident in the *Travels.*

ILL-TREATMENT OF WOMEN.—Yolked to a Plough.

Commenting on the ill-treatment of women, our author informs us, " I have frequently seen women assisting to drag a sort of light plough." Again : " In the province of *Kiangsee* nothing is more common than to see a woman drawing a kind of light plough." (p. 141.)

Now, during the progress of the embassy, through Kiangsee, Mr. Barrow sums up these extraordinary sights to a solitary instance, thus : " It was here that we saw a woman yolked literally by traces to a plough." But even this solitary instance is a mere stretch of fancy, founded, as usual, on second-hand information, which is also alluded to by Sir George Staunton, as follows : " A farmer in that province has been seen to drive, with one hand, a plough, to which his wife was yolked, while he sowed the seeds with the other hand." (II., p. 505.) How could Sir George Staunton have expressed himself in this manner if *he*, or *any* of the gentlemen, had witnessed such a sight ? And how could they have missed it, if it had been so common as the fact collector avers ? What looks rather ominous, Sir George, though treating of their progress through Kiangsee, does not say it was *here*, or in *this* province, but in " that" province, clearly indicating he was far away when the idea entered his head. Nothing more common than to see a woman yolked to the plough ! And yet this common, and, it well may be said, uncommon sight, is passed over, unnoticed, by Sir George Staunton, by Lord McCartney, and even by Anderson, whose sole object was collecting novelties. Wherever the plough drew their attention, bullocks and asses were seen yolked to it, but not a single woman. Even the subsequent English, and, still more, the Dutch embassy, which travelled twice through the famous province, and saw more of it than ever fell to the lot of *Adire Pekinum*, never witnessed such a spectacle. What judges of a popular appetite ! Nay ! had the subject matter been totally ignored a doubt might have remained, in the minds of interested sycophants, upon the ground that what was not seen by one afforded no proof that it was not seen by another. The passing observation of Sir George Staunton, however, destroys every vestige of this forlorn hope : it does more—it marshals whence the information originated.

This happens to be one of those illustrative incidents to which the individual of " acknowledged literary eminence" finds a parallel, or points to other authority to clinch his own ; unfortunately, as shown in the case of the eclipse at Tonchoo, to which the present has striking points of resemblance. At some former period, *a farmer had been seen !* and this is all the English historians know about the matter. Nevertheless, not only the Dutch embassy of one hundred and thirty years stand-

ing, but ancient Rome, itself, is raked up to assist in corroborating the "common" yet wonderful spectacle of 1793.
Strange and inscrutable, indeed, are some of the operations of
nature. The viper, for instance, irresistibly betrays itself by
its own slime. Equally irresistible are the clinching authorities
left upon the track which climbs the literary eminence, there
to remain a lasting memorial how the overgrown volume was
gorged. We wish it to be borne in mind that we hold, or
rather advocate, no opinion as to the subject matter of the
information; our object being simply to "test rigidly, by weight
and measure," the assertions so boldly put forth as the experience of the British embassy. That women were *not* seen
"yolked literally by traces to a plough" is beyond doubt; and
it is equally beyond doubt that some antiquated source originated
the hint, which, eventually, luxuriated in a spectacle than
which "nothing was more common." The idea was marvellous, and, of course, worthy the kindest regards of an author
standing ready, with outstretched arms, to welcome such *pretty
little dears*. Uneviable, indeed, must be the feelings of that
man who can ratify the marvellous statements of others, without the shadow of an evidence.

VESSEL UPSET ON RICE MILL.

However open or accessible the country might be to the
visual organs of all the imprisoned travellers, the fact collector,
every now and then, contrives to see something which the others
do not; and, it may seem over careful in us to observe what
must be self-evident, these somethings are wonderfully strange.
No doubt, he is alive to the responsibilities of his situation,
and particularly his obligations to the British public, to whom
he must give a good account of the comptrollership. He drops
down the river Longshiaton, "which by the rains was swelled
to an enormous size, and in some places had overflowed its banks,
though in general high and rocky. Several rice mills were so

completely inundated, that their thatched roofs were but just visible above the surface of the water; others were entirely washed away; and the wrecks of them scattered about the banks of the river.   A vessel of our squadron was upset upon the roof of one of these mills." (p. 532.)

Thus much we are informed, but not a word more: we are left in total ignorance as to the result of this "upset." In the name of goodness! what became of the people and property on board? Were they hurled into the raging element, and left to their fate; or what? Did our philanthropist, as on a former occasion,(*l*) exert his humanity, and insist upon the men of his barge going to the rescue? We ask these questions in vain! John Barrow, F.R.S., has introduced the catastrophe, and the reader must finish it. It is equally in vain that we call upon the other historians of the embassy: they know nothing of it—not even the "enormous flood" upon which they had embarked.(*m*) But, besides ignoring such an untoward occurrence, their statements show the utter impossibility of its ever happening. The "enormous flood" only floated with satisfaction the shallow water barges, which were changed for others of larger capacity, so soon as the water became deep enough: the overflowed banks was merely the water let in upon the rice fields; and instead of the rice mills being washed away, or just peeping above the surface of the flood, they were busy at work, and presented a very interesting sight.

As no inference is attempted, or, indeed, could be drawn from this event, unless to show the stupidity of the Chinese erecting their mills in such exposed situations, we believe it is simply a *jèu désprit*, but a most disgraceful one, founded on the rise of the river—the mere color of a pretext being enough for the "powerful motive" to rush into the marvellous.   If, instead of an "upset," however, the junk had cut a *summerset*,(*n*) on the centrifugal principle, it would have been quite as true, quite as marvellous, and saved our feelings from painful associations.   To be serious, the reader has another excellent specimen of the "facts" published under the mask of "Travels in China." An accident is alleged to have happened under circumstances that must have resulted in the most distressing consequences; yet these consequences are wholly left to conjecture. This, alone, would blast its reputation had the other narratives not rendered it an absurdity. In our humble opinion, the historian who could either invent, or ignore, such an occurrence deserves to be branded with the blackest indignation.

SPECIMENS OF EXAGGERATION.

In like manner, the Shepatan, or Eighteen cataracts, is not only the scene of numerous shipwrecks, but two or three vessels are perceived lying against the rocks, with their flat bottoms uppermost, a sight entirely unnoticed by the other journalists, who are, nevertheless, alive to the shoals and obstructions encountered in this part of the channel.(o) Altogether, our traveller is too fond of the marvellous. Besides delighting in such themes, he discovers an unconquerable disposition to run to extremes whatever he has got to work upon. A common superlative is, in general, too weak for his efforts, which must be supported on terms expressive of the most extravagant amplification. " The whirlpool, at Charybdis, could not possibly be more terrific than the tumultuous eddies boiling around Keeto point," and yet no alarm was taken. In the gulf of Pecheli, the number of small sandy islands are "prodigious,"(p) though none were seen or heard of in the track of the ships, except at the bar where they finally cast anchor. The scorpions, at Tonchoo, " crept into our beds in such numbers," though only one ventured to take a peep at the strangers, who had so unceremoniously disturbed them. " The old viceroy of Pechelee's visiting ticket contained as much crimson-colored paper as would be sufficient to cover the walls of a moderate-sized room." In the crowd at Tinghai "nothing scarcely was heard but the words *Tawhangtee* and *Hungmau*, the emperor and the Englishman;" and the pilots of the same place were "the most miserable wretches" he ever beheld. All this is outrageous exaggeration, and examples may be found in nearly every page of the so-called *Travels*. If instead of collecting "facts" the author of them had said *marvels*, the nail would have been hit upon the head, to the greatest nicety.

RASH ASSERTIONS GOOD ENOUGH FOR "FACTS."

No sort of marvel seemingly comes amiss: it is immaterial what, or whence; even an unguarded expression is laid hold of, if only sufficiently extravagant, and capable of fusion in the general scheme. Of this last circumstance there is a remarkable instance, rendered still more remarkable as being the only specimen of his own folly over which the disciple of truth has subsequently cast a slur. Anxious to acquaint his readers that he encountered one of those "tremendous gales" known by the name of typhoon, the heroic adventurer observes:

"These hurricanes sometimes blow with such strength that, according to the assertion of an experienced and intelligent commander of one of the East India Company's ships, 'Were it possible to blow ten thousand trumpets, and beat as many drums, on the forecastle of an Indiaman, in the height of a *Tafung*, neither the sound of the one nor the other would be heard by a person on the quarter-deck of the same ship.' In fact, vast numbers of Chinese vessels are lost in these heavy gales of wind; and ten or twelve thousand subjects from the port of Canton alone are reckoned to perish annually by shipwreck." (p. 41.)

The assertion of an experienced and intelligent commander is thus set forth, not only without comment, but as a forcible illustration of "these heavy gales of wind:" it is, in fine, information deserving of public confidence. In the long run, however, forth comes the darling *Auto*, tuning the gigantic merits of its illustrious parent, and, in a fit of happy humour, falls foul, not of the *Travels*, be it remembered, but of the experienced and intelligent commander who risked the rash assertion. That officer, on being doubted and questioned by our truth-devoted traveller, would not, on second thoughts, endorse what he had just uttered: nevertheless, with the knowledge of this fact, that *rash assertion*, in all its integrity, is deemed *worthy* of the *Travels*, and is spread as the experience of an intelligent commander to illustrate those tremendous gales, so fatal to Chinese seamen. Noble Mr. Barrow! exquisite collector of facts! thus did thy *reputation grow;* and thus didst thou take thy stand amongst " individuals of acknowledged eminence in science and literature:" thus, in short, didst thou open the eyes of thy benighted countrymen, who, in gratitude for the great boon, were ready to cover thee with imperishable renown! Who, then, did not envy the planet that presided at thy birth! Yet, stay! Ambition, which made Napoleon the terror of a continent, carried him on till he finished that terror on a lonely rock: even so, the same " powerful motive," which stamped the *Travels* " in a nation's eyes," hath ceased not till those *Travels* have become a proverb—a reproach! In taking his laugh out of the captain of the Hindostan, the old fool shuts his eyes to the fact that he is laughing at his own expense.(*q*)

POYANG LAKE—BARROW SWAMPS.

This disposition for the extravagant is also well illustrated in describing the desolation surrounding the Poyang lake, from which no inference is drawn, but seemingly to combat the smiling plains mentioned in Anderson's Account, a publication which has been a thorn in official quarters. The comptroller's description of the country is not very different from that of Sir George Staunton, only the desolation is of greater extent. Whenever the " two able historians " enter the same arena the former is, generally, well ahead, sometimes far; but in this instance, Jack barely beats his master.

" The nearer we approached the great lake *Poyang*, the more dreary was the appearance of the country ; and for the distance of ten miles around it, or at least on the south and west sides, was a wild waste of reeds and rank grasses, inter-rupted only by stagnant pools of water. Not a human dwelling of any description was to be seen. This place may justly be considered as the sink of China, into which rivers fall from every point of the compass. It is scarcely possible for the imagination to form to itself an idea of a more desolate region than that which surrounds the Poyang lake. The temperature was so reduced, by the circumambient waters, that on the 27th November, with drizzling showers, the thermometer was down to 48° in the forenoon. We sailed near four whole days over the same kind of country, and came towards the evening of the last, to the city of Nanchangfoo." (p. 533.)

The picture, in its present colors, is dismal, indeed ; but no sooner is the official map referred to than our wonted serenity begins to return. Upon that map, delineated by the same artist who painted the above shuddering picture, what do we find during these four memorable days? Why! three cities of the third class, three considerable towns, and a village ; all close upon the route, and so situated that a single day did not transpire without one or other being in sight : some of them even lay between the route and the dismal lake. But does the comptroller not assume a very great responsibility in attempt-ing, from his own observations, to describe the country sur-rounding a lake of such magnitude as the Poyang ? That he is determined to collect "facts" we have here the amplest evidence, and no mistake. While confident the desolation extended all round, to the distance of ten miles, he knew it was particularly so on the south, and on the west, because he had experience of it. Nevertheless, the lake was not approached nearer than ten miles, on the south only; on the west side— not at all! It lay quite beyond the visible horizon, and yet we are assured it was a " wild waste of reeds and rank grasses, where not a human dwelling of any description was to be seen."

F

To test the value of this "fact," we call upon a witness who, although not in the McCartney embassy, dare not be disputed at the present issue. The witness, now introduced, examined with his own eyes, and described with his own pen, the country all along, and close to the western shore of the Poyang lake; and as opposite as night is to day is his testimony to the "facts and observations" of the culprit. Instead of dismal swamps, "the scenery has, contrary to my anticipations, been mountainous and highly picturesque." By placing an implicit confidence in the detestable accounts of the first English embassy, the historian of the second was thus led astray. The testimony just given is, by cotemporary, and subsequent travellers, rendered an undoubted fact.

Again : had the comptroller been a merchant, and had he dealt out his commodities with the same unsparing hand, with which he measures his whims, he would not only have deserved well of the community, but been fully entitled to a niche in the temple of fame. Instead of confining his houseless desert to the vicinity of the lake, it commences while he is yet some seventy miles away. Even at this distance his eyes are stretching over the same wild waste, where not a human dwelling, of any description, was to be seen. Upon the 26th November, the first of the four memorable days, while Mr. Barrow is yearning over this awful picture of desolation, what is Lord McCartney thinking of ? Why ! he is so enraptured, at the beautifully cultivated fields, as to call out " The Chinese are surely the best husbandmen in the world." The same prospect is before both, and both are laying in their "facts" to enlighten the British public on this distant and hitherto unknown region of the world ; and what a contrast ! But has not the biographer of Lord McCartney pledged himself to the accuracy of his lordship's statements, that they were written on the ground of reality, and never afterwards interfered with on the ground of recollection ? He has done so ; and, again, we call attention to this disgusting contrast. We are almost sick of the frequency of such conflicting statements to remark that a region so inconceivably desolate should have appeared thus different to other eyes. Even Anderson, at this juncture, is as enthusiastic as his lordship, and were he alone we should prefer his statements to those of the comptroller, well satisfied that any man, even if he had not received a scholastic education, may, in a case of this nature, be quite as good a judge as the ablest linguist or mathematician.

The origin of some of the *adire Pekinum* whims is involved in considerable mystery, and their object seems inexplicable on any other ground but that of "astonishing the natives:" something marvellous must be told of the country it was the lot of few to visit. Of this class are the *Barrow Swamps*, which are always in the extreme of dismalness, without cultivation and without inhabitants. No monomaniac ever gazed with more concern on his peculiar phantasy than our author on the face of his great discovery. Not content with outraging the country that really passed in review, whole regions, lying beyond the reach of sight, must feel the weight of his desolating vengeance. Sir George Staunton, himself, though usually exercising a greater amount of caution, is not in a much better position respecting the swamps in question. He has, indeed, the assurance to tell us that the maps of the embassy " convey a faithful picture of the country, through interesting remarks made every day upon the spot." (II, p. 523.) As a specimen of these remarks the following description of the Poyang shall speak for itself.

" The whole country around this lake is nothing but a swamp for many leagues, and will admit of no kind of cultivation notwithstanding it is very populous, every dry patch of ground having a village upon it." The school in which the comptroller was taught is here examplified to a nicety ; but let us compare this " faithful picture " of the map with the faithful picture of the official volumes. " For the distance of some miles, indeed, on every side of it, the face of the country is one wild and morassy waste, covered with reeds and rushes, and entirely inundated for a part of the year. Not a village is to be seen ; nor any traces of habitation visible, except now and then a mean and solitary hut for the residence of a fisherman, so situated sometimes as to be approached only by a boat." (II, p. 497.)

Who, on comparing these "faithful pictures," could have suspected the author of the official volumes guilty of such abominable inconsistencies. By the "interesting remark," made upon the spot, the morassy waste extends to "many leagues ;" by the "Authentic Account," it dwindles down to the modest distance of "some miles." By the former—the same waste is crowded with population and villages ; by the latter—"not a village is to be seen," and scarcely the trace of a human habitation. It is not often we find the learned gentleman committing himself in this manner ; it, however, only proves that the greatest caution will sometimes overreach itself.

But had Sir George Staunton confined his interesting remarks to what really passed before his eyes, they are still a gross imposition on public opinion ; because cotemporary as well as subsequent testimony prove that no such swamps were encountered here, or indeed anywhere on the route. The country was flat and cultivated, and, though tame or poor in the eyes of some, was beautiful and fertile in the eyes of others ; but, in every instance, vastly different to the abhorrent colors of the "faithful pictures." It even appears, the Jaou country, on the south-east side of the lake, is the subject of a Chinese proverb, which observes " The habits and temper of the people are remarkable for openness and generosity, as the soil is for its productiveness, and the higher classes for education and refinement."

SANDY ISLANDS OF THE POYANG.

We are not yet done with the learned baronet, "In the lake," he tells us, "were scattered small sandy islands just peeping above the surface of the water, and covered with humble dwellings, the abodes of fishermen." (II, p. 498.)

As no other gentleman of the embassy assumes the responsibility of having seen this lake, and being fully persuaded they could not, we are tempted to ask a very simple question : At what distance, along a flat surface, could such islands be seen by a human eye ? Without putting our readers to the inconvenience of a calculation, the traveller shall be allowed to answer for himself. Approaching the mouth of the Pyho, " the coast is so very low as to be scarce discoverable, at two miles distance, but by means of the buildings erected on it." If such was the effect at two miles distance, what must have been the appearance of the small sandy islands of the Poyang, the verge of which was scarcely approached within ten miles ? Is it likely the islands, or lake, were seen at all ? But De Guignes, who soon followed in the same line, expressly states that the lake was impossible to be discovered ; and Dr. Milne, who long afterwards actually entered the lake, and sailed past these islands, describes them as hilly and picturesque. Thus every circumstance tends to confirm the disreputable basis upon which the historians of the McCartney embassy have founded their descriptions of China.

We have introduced the small sandy islands of the Poyang as a good elucidating example of the school which picks up an idea anyhow, and then contrives to work it in as derived from personal observation. In this case, as in many others, it proves exceedingly unfortunate—in a word, the fact overreaches itself by seeing what was impossible to be seen.

SINK OF CHINA.

Returning to the comptroller, we find he has no desire to let anything in the shape of a remarkable idea or expression pass him, when it can be dragged in ; it is, therefore, no wonder the " large quarto" should be inflated by so many of the observations already sufficiently circulated by the authentic volumes. Of course, it was not enough that Sir George Staunton should call the Poyang the "common sewer of China," into which rivers flow from "most points of the compass"—it must re-appear as the "sink of China," into which rivers fall from "every point of the compass." This is not exactly a plagiarism, but an improvement upon an original idea; and although a mere trifle, it is a perfect illustration of the *forte* of John Barrow, F.R.S.—the "common sewer" being changed into the "sink," and "most points," into "every point." Awkwardly enough, the lake is situated immediately on the south side of the great river Yangtse-kiang, into which it flows. Rivers entering the lake from the north would, of course, have to cross the Yangtse-kiang, by an aqueduct or tunnel, we presume, but are not informed which. Calling the lake or swamp, however, that receives only the drainage of a single province, the "sink of China," is but a puerile idea at the best.

LAKE CINING—Country with two Surfaces.

The lakes and swamps of Cining, besides a picture of scarce less desolation, present others of a still more extra-ordinary character.

"Having passed on the 26th October the walls of the city *Cining*, where a multitude of small craft were lying at anchor, we came to an extensive lake of the same name, navigated by a great number of sailing boats. From the east side of this lake the canal was separated only by an immense mound of earth. To the westward the whole country, beyond the reach of sight, was one continued swamp or morass, upon which were interspersed pools or ponds of water abounding with the nelumbium, at this time in full flower." (p. 505.)

No less than two glaring absurdities are embodied in this single extract: "The whole country, *beyond the reach of sight,* was one continued swamp or morass;" while an "extensive lake, navigated by a great number of sailing boats," occupies the same local position that is also occupied by "a continued swamp or morass, interspersed with pools of water." Dismissing for a moment these abominations, we have proof, from Sir George Staunton and the map, that the canal did *not* pass along the east side of this lake, but along the east side of another lake, approached two days afterwards. Tossing these authorities aside, and placing greater confidence in his own "loose notes," the would-be traveller seems to have jumbled them together to bring out a new idea, for he is evidently confounding the two situations. He has, however, overreached himself, and placed a continued swamp upon an extensive lake, an absurdity from which no consideration will relieve him. If he has mistaken the east for the west he has also mistaken the lakes and their adjoining peculiarities; and to thrust forward such trumpery as "Travels in China" is, to say the least of it, the height of impertinence. But there cannot be any mistake in the matter seeing the descriptions are faithfully transferred from one edition to another. It would be ridiculous to call it by any other name but ungovernable folly struggling to write a narrative, which, while pressing upon its whims like an incubus, is contemptible from first to last, even if blunders and absurdities had found no portion in it.

The whole country, where the eye could not reach, is actually described as a continued swamp abounding with the nelumbium, then "wasting its sweetness on the desert air." Nothing short of an able match for the gun that could shoot about corners must have reached and collected this observation. What an enviable telescope!(r) Who, after this, can doubt that the comptroller, on leaving England, had screwed up his determination to a pitch that would not only scour the country, but leave to future travellers the collecting of facts a hopeless case. Till, however, we have had ocular demonstration of this wonderful piece of mechanism we shall doubt its ability, and protest against the "long range." If allowed, the combat would be too unequal, and we submit at once. As far as the eye can reach we hold to be a range sufficiently ample for the most clear-sighted to describe with any pretensions to accuracy. Did Mr. Barrow mean what he says ? He did : he has only enforced, by another satisfactory example, the same incomprehensible faculty that saw and described the houseless swamps of the " sink of China."

BARROW SWAMPS OF SHANTONG.

During three days journey, or about eighty miles from Cining, the country, indeed, consisted in nothing else but lakes or swampy ground half covered with water ; and, except on the water and the islands, the *whole* of it may be said to be uninhabited, and *totally* devoid of any kind of cultivation. " Sometimes, indeed, a few miserable huts appeared on the small hillocks that here and there raised their heads out of the dreary waste of morass ; but the chief inhabitants were cranes, herons, guillemots, and a vast variety of other kinds of birds that frequent the waters and swamps."(s) (p. 507.)

By this time, we fancy our readers will not turn pale at a Barrow swamp: as usual, however, he reckons without his host ; for it can be shown, from authority which dare not be disputed, that even these eighty miles were not quite so dreary as they are painted. The " elegant and accurate" details, themselves, while doing every justice to the swamps, are not unmindful of the population and culture, abundance of both presenting themselves all along. The view, itself, never ceased to be bounded by a range of highly interesting hills. It is true, some twenty years afterwards an extensive inundation had overspread this part of the country, and laid a great portion of it under water ; but the most smiling plains have suffered from such calamities, and independent of the many towns and villages all along the canal—the trees, the picturesque situations, and traces of cultivation, proved the country as a whole to have

been anything but a dismal swamp. It is further remarkable
that the authority now relied upon, when coasting the great
Paoying lake, south of the Yellow river, observes "On the
right bank, for the first time, since leaving the country of
Tongcoo, was a tract of uncultivated ground, abandoned to
rushes and briars." Mr. Ellis, who followed in the identical
footsteps of Mr. Barrow, denies seeing a tract of uncultivated
ground from the mouth of the Pyho till south of the Yellow
river. But to show the state of the country during the three
dreary days of the McCartney embassy, and, of course, to show
the basis upon which the "fact collector" has reared his dreams
of desolation, we transcribe a few jottings from our private
journal.

"October 27. At 11, passed a flood gate. The current,
forward, has through the two or three last gates been rapid.
Lake—vast number of villages on its borders. Extensive
level fields—cutting down a tall grass or grain—short scythe—
rake of a peculiar construction. At 12, a flood gate. Long
village. Three ploughs in a field, each drawn by a bullock
and two asses; one of the asses was sucked by a young colt.
The plough has only one handle, held by the right hand, and
the reins or halter in the left; the share appeared broad and
thin, and the whole very light, but at too great a distance for
accurate inspection. Soil seems light and easy. At 1, a flood
gate. Three wheelbarrows with each a sail. At 2, a flood
gate. Large village. At 4, a town with 17 square towers:
I counted that number. It is situated at the bottom of a range
of hills, extending from north to south. Canal, here, broader
than formerly. Another flood gate. At 5, a flood gate, and
a long town, but contrived, as usual, that we should pass
through it in the dark. The town we have just passed is
very large.

"October 28. At day-light, passed a very long range of
shipping: several. boats loaded with coal. Rice grounds—
fields under water. At 1, a flood gate, and a large walled city,
the largest we have seen since leaving Tonchoo. Ships built

here.   At 4½, a narrow and shallow part of the canal.   Little
sprigs, some with red flags placed in the water to warn us of
the shallows.   The sand has made encroachments.   A cross-
cut ; open to the left, but a bank cuts off the communication
to the right.

"October 29.   On our right, a long wall separating the
canal from an extensive lake.   The wall is about five feet high,
built either of marble or granite : Dr. Gillan thinks marble.
There is a space of fifty feet of earth between the waters of
the canal and this lake.   Several openings—sluices commu-
nicating with the lake, over one of which the water fell into
the canal, from a height of three to four feet.   Several nets
hanging with the crown downwards.   At 12, current strong
in our favor.   Canal very shallow ; touching the bottom frequently, this morning—sudden turnings—seems to have been
a river, which, laying in the direction, was taken advantage of."

Such are some of the features of this dreary waste of morass,
sketched while they were in sight, and consequently free from
the distortions which a medium of ten years is so likely to
produce, even upon a conscientious mind.   From all this, supported by cotemporary and subsequent accounts, we are fully
persuaded that, instead of a boundless dreary waste of morass,
Mr. Barrow saw an extensive plain, occasionally varied with
wood and water, swamps and cultivation, towns and villages,
and always terminated by lofty picturesque mountains.   We
are also persuaded that he saw abundance of people pursuing
their various employments, and that the " cranes, herons, and
guillemots," sprung into existence exactly on the same principle
that adorned the " sink of China " with " bulrushes," and
other varieties of "rank grasses."   Being the natural concomi-
tants of such situations it is immaterial to our author whether
they were seen or not.(t)

IMMENSE AQUEDUCT.

It is certainly foreign from our purpose to enter into an

examination of the official account beyond the influence it exercises on that of the comptroller, as a check upon his assertions, or illustrative of the school in which he was trained. The same inaccuracy of detail; and the same disposition to invent and ignore, to generalize and confound, characterize the "splendid work" equally with its "valuable addition;" only the present baronet exercises great caution, and usually keeps within reasonable limits, with which the future baronet disdains to be trammelled. In both, much of the information respecting the Grand canal is either wild speculation, or derived from sources that never occurred on the embassy. On this point, a careful comparison of the map with the descriptions will of itself be satisfactory. In its progress through that part of the country now on hand, Sir George Staunton observes : " It was a curious spectacle, though not without modern examples upon a smaller scale, to see a vast body of water, forced up by human skill and industry, into a narrow channel several yards above its former bed, and flowing along in that airy state, till it finds a corresponding level at a considerable distance." (II, p. 392.) The distance surely was considerable, not less than eighty miles, if any reliance is to be placed upon the veracity of Mr. Barrow, who is equally anxious with his master to bear testimony to this great undertaking.

" To the southward, or descending part of the country, the projectors have been obliged to force up the water between immense banks of earth and stone, far above the level of the flat surface ; consisting almost entirely of lakes, swamps, and morass. The quantity of human labour that must have been employed, in amassing together the different materials that compose this immense aqueduct, could not have been supplied, in any reasonable length of time, except in a country where millions could be set to work at the nod of a despot." (p. 511.)

In tracing upon the map this work of next to superhuman skill and industry certain exceedingly awkward features present themselves at the first glance. High and airy as the vast body of water glides along, it is, nevertheless, the receptacle of

numerous streams, which flow into it from both sides.   It was
certainly worth the attention of such acute observers to have
explained how these feeders discharged themselves into a
channel so far above the common level.   Whether the accurate
draughtsman copied from the maps of the Jesuits, or whether
he threw the streams in at random, as embellishments to his
own, is immaterial: he straddles the horns of a dilemma, and
there he must remain.   In a country "flat beyond the reach of
sight," these streams and their tributaries must, necessarily,
have been banked up to the "airy" height, presenting, altogether,
an accumulation of embankments still more " gigantic" than
the canal itself, which only has found favor in his eyes.   In
vain, however, did the subsequent English embassy look for
the *wide* valley, to bridge which, these " gigantic" embankments were "forced up;" a flat surface only met their
eyes.(*u*)   The canal, itself, for certain, was fed by numerous
streams, which fell into it as they passed along, proving to a
demonstration that it was not elevated above the level of the
country.   In vain, too, did they look for the massive walls of
coarse grey marble supporting this high embankment, and well
they might, as no such walls or embankment were ever seen in
the position fixed by the " Authentic Account " of the first
English embassy.   All this is satisfactorily corroborated by
the memorandums last quoted from Dr. Dinwiddie's journal,
which, apparently, never fails to notice any remarkable embankment or excavation ; yet, on this occasion, it is silent and
significantly so.   The canal had all the appearance of a river ;
had sudden turnings, varied greatly in width, was very shallow,
and full of sand banks, indicated by little red flags.   Instead
of sluices letting down the water upon the adjacent country,
the only sluices taken notice of are those that came from the
lakes to supply the canal, into which the water fell some three
or four feet.   The truth of this last assertion carries its own
evidence in the nets which were seen hanging at these sluices.

It is worthy of remark that these hanging nets, as well as
the little red flags, are ignored by the "two able historians ;"

this much is certain—they were not very agreeable companions of an "airy" height. Neither were the cross-cut canals. Even the ignored villages and walled towns, and particularly the one with the ship-builder's yards, were unlikely spectacles on the brink of a high and narrow aqueduct. Whatever amount of strength or solidity may have been given to the banks it could only have been to resist, and not to elevate, the waters in the channel, which certainly was not higher than the adjacent country. The "immense aqueduct" is clearly a creature of the brain—another marvel; first experimented on by Sir George Staunton, and finally, by his pupil, amplified to the extravagant standard of the *Travels*.

GRAND CANAL.—"ALL THE TALENTS."

It seems doubtful if the public, even yet, possesses much reliable information respecting the details of the Grand canal, and the topography of the country through which it stretches; but whether now, or whether hereafter, the virtuoso, who may feel so interested, will find a most deplorable accumulation of nonsense in the map and descriptions furnished by the three chief writers of the British embassy. If these gentlemen were qualified they were dishonest journalists. Instead of using their pencils while moving on, they have left their observations to be decided by future reflections, based on memory and their kind friends, the Jesuits. Nothing else can account for the matchless absurdities they have committed. Confused notions of lakes and swamps, excavations and embankments, levels and currents, floodgates, sluices, and equilibrium ditches, have settled upon the brains of all; and these ideas, after being pounded in a common mass, are moulded anew, each to his taste, but no two alike. "When rogues fall out, honest men get their own," and truth, perhaps, has no reason to grumble at the dissonance of such a triumvirate. Whatever is asserted by one is almost sure to be confuted by another, while they have brushed up an old map setting themselves, one and all, at defiance. If his lordship traces the canal in the winding bed of an ancient river, the comptroller gets immediately to work, and digs down to the depth of thirty to seventy feet. If the minister plenipotentiary tries his hand at digging, then, to prove his "inveterate hatred of idleness," Mr. Barrow employs all the *barrows* of the empire in raising up his "gigantic embankments." If the same "inveterate" gentleman, to improve upon the missionaries, lays the country out into boundless, uninhabitable swamps, Sir George and his lordship, nevertheless, reserve each a favourite, though different portion, adorned with wood, water, and every feature to render a landscape beautiful. If Sir George, with the eye of genius, brings a feeder from his favored lake, his lordship immediately sinks that lake deep beneath the level of the canal; but, on the other hand, if he attempts to feed the canal from the lake he is admiring, Sir George and his pupil put their shoulders together, and up goes the "immense aqueduct" to that "airy" height which confounds his lordship, and renders his feeder unavailing. If, again, to enjoy the prospect of a boundless rushy swamp, occupying the position that is also occupied by an extensive navigable lake—if, we repeat it, to enjoy and collect this astounding "fact," the comptroller conducts the canal along the east side of lake Cining, then the ambassador, assisted by the next in command, gives a strong pull, and a "pull all together," and back it comes to its proper position on the west. Such is a feeble outline of the abominations attending an attempt to harmonize the observations before us; but when the map is brought into play, the shock, at once, becomes overwhelming, and the task has to be given up in despair.

But this jumbling is susceptible of elucidation by a much easier process—easier to be understood. When descending from the summit level, the canal passed a lake, on the left hand, and the situation, altogether, reminded Lord McCartney of the canal at Lake Lagoda, in Russia. The observations of his lordship on this occasion are faithfully transferred by Sir George Staunton to another lake passed some days afterwards, and which lay on the contrary, or right side of the canal. (II, p. 398) The descriptions in our manuscript journal, while giving every countenance to those of his lordship, show the scenery of the two situations to have been very different : nevertheless, the author of the Authentic Account has thought proper to elucidate the one locality by observations written expressly for the other. How, after this, is it possible to expect correct information flowing from such contaminated sources ! On a certain occasion, the comptroller mentions with seeming regret his ignorance of the school to which one of his colleagues belonged. Verily ! we have not much reason to congratulate him on the school of Sir George Staunton. Little, indeed, did the master think he was teaching the young idea that was, one day, destined to far outshoot his own cautious calculations, and be the means of laying the whole imposture bare.

GRAND CANAL.—Mr. Barrow's "Endeavor."

Having seen the consequences resulting from the combined efforts of " all the talents," let the reader revert to the comptroller alone, and take a peep at his " endeavor."

" I shall endeavor to convey, in a few words, a general idea of the principles on which this grand undertaking has been carried on. All the rivers of note in China fall from the high lands of Tartary, which lie to the northward of Thibet, crossing the plains of this empire in their descent to the sea from west to east. The inland navigation being carried from north to south cuts these rivers at right angles, the smaller streams of which terminating in it afford a constant supply of water ; and the three great rivers, the *Euho(v)* to the north, the *Yellow river* towards the middle, and the *Yangtsekiang* to the south, intersecting the canal, carry off the superfluous water to the sea. The former, therefore, are the *feeders*, and the latter the *dischargers* of the great trunk of the canal. A number of difficulties must have arisen in accommodating the general level of the canal to the several levels of the feeding streams; for notwithstanding all the favorable circumstances of the face of the country, it has been found necessary in many places to cut down to the depth of sixty or seventy feet below the surface ; and in others, to raise mounds of earth upon lakes and swamps and marshy grounds, of such a length and magnitude that nothing short of the absolute command over multitudes could have accomplished an undertaking, whose immensity is only exceeded by the great wall." (p. 336.)

Unable to resist the propensity to sweeping assertions, *all* the rivers of note in China must fall from the high lands of Tartary, notwithstanding the Sekiang and many others do not make the slightest approach to that central part of the continent: even the Euho, one of the notables mentioned by name, lies wholly within the ancient provinces, to one of which it is all but confined. But the Yellow and Blue rivers, themselves, though twisted to our author's purpose, have their sources more properly in Thibet, and the *only* "river of note," that really satisfies the assumptions of the "endeavor," is the Amour ; but so far from cutting this, or even the Sekiang, at right angles, the canal claims no connexion with either by many hundreds of miles. Admitting, however, all this to have been described with "equal elegance and accuracy"—that *every* river of note," in China, truly descended from the Tartarian bulges, and was actually cut at right angles by the inland navigation — admitting all this — Where do the "smaller streams" come from ; or to what are they allied ? If they are not the relatives of the "right angles," what are they? What is the meaning of the "which;" or to what has that pronoun reference ? But, again; admitting the "smaller streams" also to have been described with "equal elegance and accuracy," and every particular rendered as clear as a noon-day sun,— how is it that, in order to accommodate the level to these feeders, the Chinese have been obliged to "force up" the canal between gigantic embankments of such length and magnitude that their immensity is exceeded only by the great wall ? Is it a necessary consequence, in levelling, that the recipient should thus be elevated above its feeders, according to the philosophy of the *uncommon lot*. From its commencement at Cining, till it merges in the Yellow river, the "immense aqueduct," whether " several feet above,"—" considerably above," —or " far above," never once subsides to the general level of the country, nor gives a single feeder an opportunity of discharging itself, unless on some hydrodynamic principle peculiar to the region of marvels.

But the difficulties do not end here: every feature, attempted to be explained, is either enveloped in mystery,—attended with inconsistency,—or it is opposed to well-ascertained facts ; and yet, we are assured, all this is an "endeavor to convey, in a few words, a general idea of the principle on which this grand undertaking has been carried on." The "endeavor," truly, is a remarkable one, embodying as it does a greater amount of insipid nonsense than, perhaps, is to be found anywhere else, in the same number of lines. Nevertheless, the review, which pronounced the ablest sentence on the *Travels*, stamped the descriptions of the Grand canal as "faithfully recorded,"— as the "best part of the work ;" and, still later, one of our most entertaining cereals laid hold of the "endeavor" to illustrate the canals of China. Praiseworthy as many of these attempts are in giving a wide berth to the knowledge and experience of able and interesting writers, it surely, nevertheless, becomes the duty of those who are thus engaged to know the meaning of the borrowed language, and its applicability to the purpose on hand. The "endeavor," being the sentiments of an author of reputation, is, evidently, taken for granted as having some meaning, and, as a matter of consequence, a reader with ample brains is supposed to find it out.

UNIFORM OF KIANGNAN.

The shifts to which the historians of the McCartney embassy have been driven for materials, sometimes, seem miserable indeed. " As soon as the yachts had entered into the province of Kiangnan, a mark of attention was paid to the embassy by the viceroy there, which had not been thought of before. The trackers employed upon the Peiho, at the entrance of the ambassador into China, and hitherto on his return, were clad in the plain blue cotton garments, and sometimes indeed in the tattered remnants of the poorest peasantry. They now appeared in a new and regular uniform, edged with red, and a smart bonnet with a flat red button on the top of it, all of which passed from one set of trackers to another." (II, p. 415.)

So says the master, and wherever he luxuriates the pupil dashes to the same feast as common property; but either through ignorance, or recklessness, he applies the food to a very different purpose: thus—

" The greater the distance from the capital, the better was the apparent condition of the people. The viceroy, when he received his excellency on the entry of the embassy into this province, happened to cast his eye upon the half starved and half naked trackers of the boats; and being either ashamed of their miserable appearance, or feeling compassion for their situation, he ordered every man immediately a suit of new cloaths." (p. 562.)

Thus, the pupil would persuade us the " suit of new cloaths" was the gift of compassion, when his master affirmed it was to honor the embassy, and that the uniform passed from one set of trackers to another. It happens well that the " lot of going to Pekin" has not been confined to the Stauntons and the Barrows alone : the coy dame has also smiled on others of an opposite school, and it appears that the uniform of Kiangnan is an "immemorial usage" of the province, on state occasions. On entering the province the trackers were robed in their insignia ; and again disrobed at the other threshold, of all which we should have been left in ignorance, but for the accounts of the Amherst embassy. Thus an ancient custom, through ignorance and artifice, is twisted by the two authors to very different purposes. By one—it is a mark of respect to the embassy; by the other—a mark of compassion for the miserable wretches, and in which the author of it sees a proof of the progressive improvement of the condition of the people. The reasoning is Barrow-like. "The greater the distance from the capital the better was the apparent condition of the people," and this is proved by the viceroy's compassion for the half starved, half naked trackers, presenting them with a uniform, which nevertheless, is asserted to have passed from one set of trackers to another.

SOOCHOO BEAUTIES.

The observations and whims on woman alone have assisted materially in swelling out the "large quarto," and this is rather extraordinary considering the want of opportunities; but even with this exuberance we should not have quarrelled had the subject been conducted with consistency, a quality only found in our author in connection with his constancy to contradiction. In this respect he is uniformly consistent. But to our purpose: when the embassy was drawing to a close, and had reached Chauchoo, in the province of Canton, some ferry girls arrested attention in the travellers, and we have the following remarkable confession.

"Having for so great a length of time scarcely ever set our eyes upon a female, except the heads of some at a distance, peeping from behind the mud walls that surround the houses, or laboring in the grounds of *Kiangsee*, the ferry girls, though in reality very plain and coarse featured, were considered as the most beautiful objects that had occurred in the whole journey." (p. 595.)

When tested by other accounts, there is some truth in the

foregoing extract, viz : few women, comparatively, were seen, and these generally at a distance. But after such an admission, what are we to make of the same author's observations at Saupoo and Soochoo, the latter place in particular, where " the numerous inhabitants that appeared upon and without the walls of this extensive city, were better dressed and said to be more contented and cheerful, than we had yet observed them in any other place. For the most part they were cloathed in silk. The ladies were here dressed in petticoats, and not in trowsers, as they had hitherto appeared to the northward. The general fashion of the head dress was a black satin cap with a triangular peak, the point descending to the root of the nose, in the middle of which, or about the centre of the forehead,(w) was a crystal button. The whole face and neck were washed with a preparation of white lead, and the cheeks highly rouged; and two vermillion spots, like wafers, were particularly conspicuous, one on the centre of the under lip, and the other on the chin. Their feet were universally squeezed down to an unnatural size. Few females were seen among the immense crowds that the novelty of the sight had brought together, but great numbers had assembled in the houses, and particularly on board the pleasure and passage yachts, with the intention of satisfying their curiosity. The superior style of dress and the appearance of the women in public at this place, so different from the general custom of the country, could only be explained by the writings of the missionaries." (p. 517.)

Surely such an assemblage of well dressed, handsome ladies, gratifying curiosity at the passing strangers, was a far more beautiful sight than the plain, coarse featured ferry girls of Chauchoo. How, then, has the Soochoo beauties been so soon forgotten ? Nay ! our author distinctly denies seeing them, the only exceptions to the ferry girls being the laboring women of Kiangsee, and those peeping from behind the mud walls, in the northern districts. These, we are assured, were the *only exceptions* in the whole journey. Alas ! we find the comptroller has been taking another lesson from the missionaries,

whose writings only could explain the cause of so interesting
an improvement at Soochoo, where, we fear, this great con-
course of female beauties has been, purposely, contrived to
bear out those very explanations. And we fear also the
writings of the missionaries only can explain the phenomena
of the *telescope*, to the powers of which there seem to have
been no limits. Nothing, in fact, was safe from its penetrating
search; even brick and mortar afforded no security. Whether
the women were peeping from behind mud walls, at a distance,
or looking out from the windows, our admirable traveller
could see "their feet were universally squeezed down to an
unnatural size."

The speculations of the comptroller, like the children of
iniquity, are born to trouble: some drag or other always hangs
upon them, and there is rather a remarkable one in the present
case. Lord McCartney informs us the embassy passed through
Soochoo in the evening, and this is confirmed by Dr. Dinwiddie's journal; it is even countenanced by the "faithful
pictures" of the official map. It appears the embassy
approached the suburbs of the famous city at 4 P.M. If then
the sun set that evening directly after five, as it did, and if the
yachts took three and a half hours in reaching the city walls,
as the comptroller affirms, a tolerable estimate may be formed
of the light whose benign influence was shed on this interesting
occasion. The moon was too young to be of any service, but,
to give the culprit every due advantage, it must be borne in
mind that a "feast of lanterns" always attended the embassy
when passing a city after the shades of evening had descended.
Illuminated by such a feast only could the walls of Soochoo be
crowded by its well-to-do inhabitants, and the windows and
pleasure yachts be thronged by its female beauties; and by
such a feast only could our author scrutinize the "superior
style of dress," the "rouged cheeks," and the "cheerful
countenances," all of which cut so deep that he was enabled to
paint the charming picture after ten long years. Here is a
"fact" for England! but—tell it not in Gath! publish it

not in the streets of Ascalon the awkward hour when all this happened! an hour which at once explains and corroborates the observations on the Chauchoo ferry girls.

But this highly-favored city has even bewildered Sir George Staunton, who, according to the regime of his school, has, here, reproduced the identical observations of Lord McCartney written for the city of Chanchoo, which, with other places of a similar character, was passed in broad day-light. Though rustling in silks, and adorned with fair complexions, these cities, unfortunately, had not been rendered famous; and instead of spending their powder on such small game the wily travellers reserved it for the " bird of paradise," which was at hand.

LAKE TAIHOO.

From exactly the same sources is Lake Taihoo discovered to be celebrated for its fish and picturesque scenery, and our diligent traveller, wishing to add to his " facts," naturally enough proposes a party to so desirable a retreat; but the good-natured Van would not, on this occasion, consent. Granting such an outrageous proposal to have been made, how could the conductor consent to it, if the lake was at the distance represented on the carefully constructed map, not less than ten miles? And what a keen observer must the minister plenipotentiary have been? In direct violation of the laws of nature, the distance, intervening objects, and the shadows of night, he undertakes to describe the pleasure barges sailing upon the lake, and the interesting accommodations afforded by the female rowers: his penetration even reached the picturesque beauties on the opposite shore some thirty miles away, according to the map, whose accuracy was beyond all doubt. The observations, indeed, are an insult to common sense, even if it had been broad day-light, and the shores of the lake at no greater distance than a mile. But it cannot be discovered that the lake was seen at all, either on the present, or on the Dutch embassy, which possessed infinitely better opportunities. No individual takes it upon him to say he saw it in reality; it is only, like the Poyang, discernible through a Staunton-Barrow mist as lying to the west, and at a short distance from Soochoo. These short distances may, however, be estimated from the circumstance of Kintechin, the famous porcelain manufactory, when over a hundred and thirty miles from the travellers' route, was considered as "not very far": a willing eye will indeed reach to great distances. The whole drift of all this lies in a nut shell. The missionaries, and other writers on China, were ransacked, either before, or during the compilation of the official account, and every place of note, lying in or near the route of the embassy, has been carefully stored to render the narrative entertaining, and give it a "wise-like" appearance.(x) It is immaterial whether these places were, or were not, accessible to the reach of sight; they must appear so, and something must be said about them. This is the sole foundation of the Soochoo and many other speculations; it is nevertheless disgraceful to find information thus picked up repeated as the experience of the embassy. However barren of interest, a candid narrative would have reflected greater honor than such repetitions, which offer a poor apology for the paucity of materials. When, indeed, the detestable whims and speculations have been thoroughly sifted, we believe there is more reliable information of the state of the country, as seen on the journey, to be found in the unpretending and much abused octavo of Anderson, than in the ponderous quartos of the minister plenipotentiary, with that of his pupil thrown into the same scale.

TRIFLING NOTABILIA.

In ferreting out *Notabilia*, the comptroller has alighted on some two or three spots seemingly overlooked by Sir George

Staunton, or, perhaps, deemed beneath his notice. Thus the
embassy is made to stop at Nanchang, where the anxious
traveller, in the prosecution of his inquiries, is "told" there
is a famous temple associated with a strange well. Of course,
instead of giving us some correct and useful information of
this large city, and the country in which it stands, he rushes,
at once, to the temple, and its marvellous associations, as
being of more importance. As usual, we find the embassy did
not stop at Nanchang, but passed on to a village, four miles
from it. In a similar way, when approaching the Yellow
River, the village of Senmee is "pointed out" to him, in
connexion with a curious tradition of the Astronomer Heu.
If it was worth our author's consideration to notice such a
place in the *Travels*, it was equally worth pointing out on the
"faithful" map, but neglecting to do so leaves room for doubt
as to when he acquired the knowledge of Senmee and its
traditionary associations. In this manner, the fact collector,
instead of collecting facts, will shirk the objects before him,
and fly off to wherever *notabilia* or marvellous associations
present themselves. Consequently, we have whole treatises on
ancient rebellions, inundations, famines, pestilence, and such
like, occupying the records which should have been devoted to
passing events and surrounding objects : all clearly demonstrating the missionaries and other writers were the grounds
he travelled over, and not the country itself, which, in truth,
was a sealed letter, notwithstanding it was his lot to go to
Pekin.

SHINGMOO.

Among the numerous lucubrations on Chinese theology,
occurs the following notice of Shingmoo, styled the goddess of
intelligence :

"In China, few temples are without some representation of
the nelumbium ; sometimes the Shingmoo is painted as
standing upon its leaves in the midst of a lake. In one temple

I observed the intelligent mother sitting upon the broad pellate leaf of this plant, which had been hewn out of the living rock." (p. 474.)

Besides concealing the name of the temple, our author would lead his readers to believe that visiting temples was an ordinary occurrence ; he has, however, mentioned the whereabouts in the narrative, that inscrutable check upon his speculations. At the rock of Quansin, on the Pekiang river, the embassy halted to explore an excavated temple of Poosa. " In the centre of this apartment sat the goddess Poosa upon a kind of altar, constituting a part of the rock, and hewn into the shape of the *lienwha* or nelumbium." (p. 596.)

Instead of the Shingmoo, then, it was Poosa, a very different deity, even according to our author's interpretation ; adding another to the many proofs that the same circumstance twice alluded to exposes some reckless disregard of truth.(*y*)

So far for Barrow versus Barrow : but his lordship, who also inspected this souterrain, paints the deity in vastly different colors. "Here the god Pusa is displayed in all his glory, a gigantic image with a Saracen face grinning horribly from a double row of gilded fangs, a crown upon his head, a naked cimetar in one hand, and a firebrand in the other."

Is not this remarkable ? Both call the excavation a temple of Poosa (or Pusa,) and both describe the deity from which the temple takes its name ; yet mark the contrast ! the one— a terrible gigantic male ; the other—a gentle female deity. It is true, the comptroller makes an attempt at reconciliation, by enveloping the place in one of his mysterious fogs, in which he cunningly contrives to introduce the shadow of another deity to bear out his lordship's descriptions. But it is in vain : there were only two stories, and Lord McCartney, who minutely inspected all the apartments, leaves not a spot for Mr. Barrow to place his "intelligent mother" either sitting or standing. It is, moreover, as clear as the sun at noon day that she is made to occupy the centre of the very hall that was already occupied by the terrible god.(*z*)

PARKER'S LENS.

In the former part of this inquiry we had occasion to speak of Parker's great lens, and we now recur to the subject for some further comment. The *Travels* observes : " The only inquiry they made about it was, whether the substance was crystal ; but being informed it was glass, they turned away with a sort of disdain, as if they would say, Is a lump of glass a proper present to offer to our great *Whangtee ?* " (p. 342.)

Let the reader compare this extract with its dubious brother from Lord McCartney's journal, already quoted in this inquiry, (p. 35) and mark the discrepancies in detailing a transaction that involved no cause for discrepancies. If the Chinese turned away in disdain on learning to their *only* inquiry that the lens was a lump of glass, why should they manifest such anxiety to see it fixed and tested ? How is it they also asked Mr. Barrow whether he could not make such another for them ? And again : mark the voluminous, equivocal answer returned to the plain question of the Chinese ! " It was made by the artist who had executed the lustres, and whose sole profession was to compose works of glass and crystal, and that there was not such another lens in the world besides." He would not commit himself by saying whether he could, or could not. The same question is also put to Dr. Gillan, and, moved by the same spirit, he returns a similar answer, "There was not such another in the world besides." He likewise did not commit himself ; and, surprisingly enough, this absurd answer seemed to satisfy the Chinese. Satisfy them of what ! whether Mr. Barrow could, or could not, make them such another lens. Most assuredly, it would not have satisfied us. It is a bombastic evasion of a simple question, and involves no little amount of self-consequence, because the glaring fact was staring him in the face that he could not erect the lens, much less manufacture one. What a figure must he have assumed when Dr. Dinwiddie stepped in upon his futile attempts ! So far from putting such questions, we fancy the Chinese, observ-

ing the *bustle* he was in, looked upon him in a very different
light ; and if they offered a hundred or two hundred hands to
assist him—it must have been ironically so. We have proof
they were not insensible to fun when, at the erection of the
planetarium, " the men were told they labored much and did
nothing."

Truth occasionally ooses out from among these abominable
speculations, only it is not self-evident till the proper test be
applied. For instance : it is true the Chinese had a poor
opinion of works in glass, as the lustres and lens equally
testified. In the last extract, from the *Travels*, this is fully
substantiated by the comptroller observing, " Is a lump of glass
a proper present to offer to our great Whangtee ? " Notwithstanding, the same comptroller, whose consistency consists in
being inconsistent, never once alludes to the fate of these
remarkable works of English art. Neither does Sir George
Staunton, who is so illiberal as to try his best to create a
different impression from the truth. While informing us that
the beautiful lustres were shifted with great adroitness by
Chinese workmen, we are left in total darkness that they were
stowed away in an outside apartment, as useless. The same
" two able writers" are no less silent on the fate of the lens'
house, which, no doubt, with equal adroitness, was taken to
pieces, and the two lenses laid upon the pavement of the court.
These facts were patent both to Mr. Barrow and Sir George
Staunton ; yet mark their disingenuous attempts at con-
cealment. The former, indeed, admits the lens " excited no
admiration," while the latter was of opinion, " It could
scarcely escape the philosopical mind of his imperial majesty,
that the same material, glass, was made to operate, by
European ingenuity, such various and extraordinary purposes."
(II, p. 324.) Writing in this shameless manner, when he
knew that the emperor had treated the instruments as we have
shown, is enough to throw the odium of disgrace upon the
whole narrative. How different is the sentiments of Dr.
Dinwiddie at this unfortunate issue. " That lens, of which

there is not an equal in the world, is consigned to everlasting oblivion."

GARDENS OF YUEN-MIN-YUEN.

Occasionally scattered in the official volumes, the "facts and observations," of the "interesting episode," may be picked up; and when confronted with the *Travels*, the same contradictory consequences follow, confirming the *baseless foundations* of the "unbiassed conclusions." Thus: the gardens of Yuen-min-yuen are the subject of great eulogy in the "Splendid Account," which quotes from Mr. Barrow, who "thought it a delightful place." (II, p. 306.) This idea is much dwelt upon in a generalized description of the various beauties composing the imperial paradise. In the *Travels*, however, the same Mr. Barrow is not quite so enthusiastic as he was when drawing up, or rather endorsing, the flattering paragraph just alluded to, and he sums up his opinion thus: "They fall very short of the fanciful and extravagant descriptions that Sir William Chambers has given of Chinese gardening. Much, however, has been done, and nothing that I saw could be considered as an offence to nature." (p. 123.)

Certainly not! a blind man, who had never been in China, could have unbosomed his sentiments with equal propriety. Instead of the allusions to Sir William Chambers, it would have been quite as near to the purpose to have remarked that they fall very short of the fanciful and extravagant descriptions that I gave to Sir George Staunton; for it is certainly throwing cold water on the place previously considered "delightful." A glimmering of shame seems to pervade this acknowledgment; at all events, it is another instance of the change of sentiment brought about by the light which the Dutch embassy threw upon the subject. This is the more apparent from the remarkable discrepancy respecting the extent of these gardens as furnished by our author on the two occasions. When the paragraph was concocted for Sir George Staunton, " the circuit is not less than twelve miles," but when the *Travels* made their appearance, the same ground is inflated to " at least ten miles in diameter ;" (p. 122) or, being square, to something like forty miles in circuit ; in short, to more than nine times its former extent.(*aa*) The proprietor could have had no reason to grumble at such an increase in ten years. But how significant ! the proceedings of the Dutch embassy appeared in the mean time, and, while moderating their beauties, amplified the extent of these gardens beyond anything ever dreamed of in the philosophy of the fact collector. Aware the Dutch possessed some opportunities for judging, which he never did, he has judiciously, or it may be injudiciously, (we scarce know which) assimilated his views to theirs. Like himself, however, he neither acknowledges it, nor explains how he insulted the world by two such widely different estimates.

The comptroller's readiness to describe these gardens, while combining some attempts at absurdity, discloses the very feelings of a disappointed candidate ; but it is unnecessary. No reasonable man would blame him for not effecting what was beyond his control. How was it possible for a prisoner, who could not stir a foot without being pursued, to form any idea either as to beauty or extent. But he knew, or, more probably, learned afterwards, that they were *famous*, and, consequently, something must be said about them. We thus find this paradise summed up to certain features peculiar to all Chinese gardening, which, coupled with conjecture, formed the only opportunity, and the fact collector might well say, " nothing that *I saw* could be considered as an offence to nature."

It is truly ridiculous to find Sir George Staunton, from his own experience, looking with something like step-dame eye upon the imperial gardens at Gehol, and, on the authority of Mr. Barrow, praising those of Yuen-min-yuen as " delightful ;" while the veritable Mr. Barrow, having thrown cold water on his experience at Yuen-min-yuen, extols the gardens of Gehol, on the authority of those who saw them, "as almost unrivalled for beauty, sublimity, and amenity." In himself, the fact collector has here caught a fact which evidently proves a Tartar; and, altogether, this sweet morsel looks like an able attempt to place the capstone on the climax of sophistry.

But these gardens are brimful of edification. "Unrivalled" as those of Gehol were for "beauty and sublimity," they appear, after all, to have dwindled down into insignificance when compared with the "natural and artificial beauties" of lake Seho, which, we are assured, "far exceeded anything we had hitherto "had an opportunity of seeing in China." (p. 521.)

Some of the "facts and observations" have indeed this very remarkable peculiarity, viz: however high or extraordinary in degree the first specimen may appear, it will be surpassed by the next *sui generis*. Thus the gardens of Yuen-min-yuen, although a "delightful place," grows pale before the "unrivalled beauties" of Gehol; which, in their turn, must hide their diminished heads in presence of the "far exceeding" beauties of lake Seho. At Tiensin, too, the feast provided by the governor of Pechelee was "most magnificent," for richness and variety, and yet inferior to the dinner on lake Seho which "consisted of at least a hundred dishes in succession." But all this again yields to the private entertainment on the river at Canton, where the supper, "for number and variety of dishes, exceeded anything I had hitherto met with in the country." (p. 192.) Equally so; districts were traversed where the population was found to be "excessive"—"vast"—and "immense;" nevertheless, another turned up putting them all to the route, as it proved to be "*by far* the most populous seen on the whole journey."(*bb*)   (p. 583.)

PEDESTRIAN FEAT.

In speaking of contradictions we trust our readers under-stand the matter clearly. The contradiction is not always direct, but sometimes implied ; as in the Gardens of Yuen-min-yuen. But we shall illustrate it again by another morsel picked up at random from the *Auto*. We there read, " Having now in my remarks gone rapidly and slightly over a long journey by water and land of some twelve or thirteen hundred miles through the heart of the Chinese empire ; and having walked from curiosity, as well as for the sake of making observations, not less certainly than one-tenth part of that distance," &c. (p. 115.)

Having written the above, and before he was many days older (judging from the number of pages) our author writes again of this performance ; " As a pedestrian, I travelled a full thousand miles in China." Now the reader will see it is not a contradiction in terms : a thousand miles, most assuredly, is not less than a tenth-part of thirteen hundred miles. Still a contradiction is implied, and a very remarkable one too. But even on another occasion this same pedestrian feat is set down at " several hundred miles ; " and there is little doubt that a hundred different editions would have produced exactly a hundred different results.

GLACIS ON THE GRAND CANAL.

As the Gardens of Yuen-min-yuen illustrate the improvement which the *Travels* have made upon the " Authentic Account," just so, other examples illustrate the improvement which the *Auto* has made upon the *Travels ;* all clearly demonstrating that better views are acquired as the distance in time increases. But to prevent anything in the shape of a doubt remaining on the mind of even one reader we select another specimen which will scatter that doubt in all directions.

" But to take a glance at the construction of the canal between the two mighty rivers of China :—Here, and in other places where the varied surface of the country required great changes in the levels of the canal, a succession of dams separates the two levels in the form of a glacis, of which the following sketch may serve to give an idea."(*cc*)   (p. 100.)

By the above extract, the fact collector, to prove his "effective zeal in promoting the progress of science," places upon the Grand canal a mode of navigation that did not exist thereon ; neither between the two mighty rivers, nor in any other part. The introduction of the glacis on canals was experienced only by the party who separated from the embassy at Hanchoo, and travelled to Chusan : nowhere else. The comptroller was not of that' party, and never saw such a contrivance ; and but for the Chusan travellers the glacis would have been a sealed letter. The "powerful motive," however, in one of its ablest efforts, has whipped up the contrivance and characteristically thrust it down upon the Grand canal. By so doing a double *faux pas* is committed : the glacis is placed where it did not exist ; and it is brought forward as a "fact" collected by our author, himself. To such ridiculous points of view does ungovernable vanity sometimes carry its owner.

Some account of the glacis also occurs in the *Travels*, where our author is a little more cautious of his sentiments, but equally unwilling to say how he came by the knowledge. This trifle, itself, is indicative of the selfishness of the traveller, and of his ambition to spread the information of others as his own. However, as might have been expected, the "faithful record" in the *Travels* gives a flat denial to the record, *equally faithful* we presume, in the *Auto*, respecting the glacis ; for it says "There is not a lock, nor, except these, (floodgates) a single interruption to a continued navigation of six hundred miles," (p. 337) embracing of course the space between the two mighty rivers.

ACCOMMODATION BAY.

Another improvement upon the grand inland navigation of China, quite as able as the last, but involving a principle peculiar to itself, is also brought to light by the *Auto*, thus :

" In one place the projectors of the canal had apparently deviated from the direct line to obtain an immediate communication with an extensive lake, the object of which was, as we soon found, to give to the canal the advantage of a large bay for the accommodation of shipping requiring to pass and repass its mouth at the junction of the Yellow river." (p. 96.)

The deviation alluded to is anything but apparent on the map, and we are sure that those only who possess the eyes of a Barrow could make it out. However, if there is any meaning in the above extract it is this : the canal, for commercial purposes, communicated with a lake, which, in its turn, communicated with the Yellow river. Whether the latter part of the sentence be satisfactory or not the former is so, without doubt. How, or when, our author acquired this idea may be useless to discuss; it was not, however, till long after the return of the embassy : even the last edition of the " large quarto" repudiates all knowledge of it. So does the official and other accounts of the McCartney and Amherst missions ; and if it is to be found in any writer on this great inland navigation—it could only be as an idea, not as an established fact. It appears to us " an original," picked up from studying the geographical position of the lake, the canal, and the Yellow river. Their connexion might seem a natural one, and, in all probability, has been pondered over till the " powerful motive" has not only reduced it to a reality, but added it to the " facts" collected on the British mission.

But the *Travels*, again, are inexorable, and this noble " fact," of after years, is crushed beneath the weight of other facts that are piled upon it. Although unnamed, there is no mistaking the position of the lake amid the dreary swamps where the *Travels* have " forced up" that immense aqueduct which puts human comprehension to a stretch. From this " airy" situation, so " far above the level of the flat surface," the shipping at once is launched down upon the accommodation bay, with what wisdom our readers must judge for themselves : they must even guess if recourse is had to the glacis, so

injudiciously fixed where it was not required. Altogether this
beautiful conception is worth the attention of virtuosi interested
in literary curiosities.   An idea, some fifty years before it
was born, is, at an opportune moment, made to flash upon the
minds of the British travellers, who, nevertheless, move on,
unconscious of the illumination ; and having executed its
mission, the same idea plunges back into the bosom of
forgetfulness, which, in reality, it has never left, there to
remain in its primeval nonentity till fate assigns an existence
to it in the *Auto*. A single step, it has been said, leads from
the sublime to the ridiculous : in other words, from " an
eminence in literature, to a gulf in absurdity."   Mounted on
unbridled vanity, with the cautious precepts of the master
flying in the winds, the reckless pupil scales the " literary
eminence," notwithstanding ; but, unwilling to remain there,
while " facts" are in request, and while the " progress of science
can be promoted," he, again, dashes forward into the most
benighted regions of speculation, and thus eventually plunges
headlong into the worst kind of Barrow swamps.

CHINESE ROADS.

   That Mr. Barrow did possess " an inveterate hatred of
idleness," is, at least, justified by the diligence he has
bestowed on the improvement of his " facts and observations."
The greatest attention, undeniably, has been given to this
object, and the experience of 1793 has accordingly varied its
colors as subsequent whims or information could be united to
it.   Several of the latest examples illustrate this " inveterate"
assiduity: equally so do the roads adjoining Pekin, to which
we now draw attention.   At the period of the McCartney
embassy, these roads were found in such good condition as to
draw the attention of every one, the comptroller not excepted.
Absurdly enough, it is true, while speaking with contempt of
Chinese roads, generally, the *Travels* admit those in the

environs of Pekin as "good." Nevertheless, the *Auto*, in flat
contradiction, affirms they found the roads "bad," both before
and after passing through the capital. The same irresistible
motive which induced the collector of facts to corroborate his
eclipse at Tonchoo, by the experience of the Dutch embassy,
has induced him to try a similar experiment respecting the
roads, the bad state of which is clinched by the experience of
Lord Amherst's mission. The infatuation is truly wonderful!
Our traveller will not confirm the simple and well known fact
that Lord McCartney found these roads in good condition,
although they were in a state of ruin at the arrival of Lord
Amherst. Instead of admitting so obvious a consequence, the
author of the *Travels* sees what he fancies a little assistance to
his detestable whims on the roads of China, and hence the
experience of 1793 is made to square with future discoveries,
which can never come too late ; they will be tacked to, some
how or other. A wise man, unquestionably, will look out for
improvements, but a fool only will apply them where they are
evidently worthless.

As a whole, the whims on Chinese roads are hardly inferior
to the swamps. "Except near the capital, and in some few
places where the junction of the grand canal with navigable
rivers is interrupted by mountainous ground, there is scarcely
a road in the whole country that can be ranked beyond a footpath." (p. 513.)

Here, again, the incomprehensible telescope is at work, not
only sweeping the country, but detecting obstructions from
mountainous ground that was never seen by any other traveller.
The only interruptions between the Grand canal and a navigable
river, was the few miles of flat country through the suburbs of
Hanchoo. Afterwards, two interruptions did occur from mountainous ground between one navigable river and another, but
never with the canal. However, with the little experience our
enviable traveller had of the roads of this vast empire he rushes
to one of the most insane conclusions that ever entered the
head of a man pretending to common sense. If his conclusions

are altogether founded on his own observations, how dares he
to interfere with the rest of China ?   But if he will do so, how
could he arrive at such a conclusion ?   His experience, such
as it was, was fertile of good roads, and reasoning from analogy,
was presumptive of good roads in other districts ; but instead
of this he arrives, or pretends to arrive, at the conclusion that
beyond what he saw there was not another road, in all China,
that could be " ranked beyond a footpath."   Exquisite reasoning ! beautiful support of unbiassed conclusions !   It is inconceivable how the idea got into his head at all, unless he picked
it up from the Dutch, who give a rather unfavorable account
of some of the roads, over which they travelled.   This only
seems to account for another brainless whim ; and, then,
it is upon the Dutch experience, and not his own, that the
" unbiassed conclusions are founded."   But the more we
investigate the more are we satisfied that our author was not
quite such a fool as he would lead us to believe ; it is, indeed,
impossible he could have arrived at, or have put the slightest
faith in any such conclusions.   Whatever may have given the
hint for the *swamps*, *roads*, and other whims, carried to such
extravagance, it is beyond doubt that a delight of imposing on
mankind is at the bottom of them.   China had been the theme
of many marvellous relations ; it was then, and was likely to
continue in a great measure inaccessible to Europeans ; and
these inducements, operating on a load of vanity, has resulted
in the " phantastic tricks " we are now exposing to the light.

SPECIMENS OF REMARKABLE OBSERVATION.

Most other travellers, prejudiced, splenetic, accommodating,
or whatever their dispositions, usually confine their " facts and
observations" to the reach of sight, or the vicinity of their
travels ; but it is otherwise with the Barrow-school.(*dd*)   Of
course, the same faculties which could see no roads beyond a
footpath in the " whole country " would not be at a loss to see

anything that was desirable to be seen. In consequence, we find, "There are no inns in any part of this vast empire."— "Not a decent place of retirement in all China."—"Not a vestige of a carriage to be found amongst them."—"Nor a statue, a pillar, nor a column, in the whole empire."—"In fact there are no great farms in all China,"—"and terrace cultivation is on so small a scale as not to deserve notice."— "Horses, too, scarce, small, and miserable, a remark which applies to every province of the empire." All these, and a thousand similar discoveries, swept from the length and breadth of the land, are collected during a flying journey from Pekin to Canton, and while the *fact collector*, himself, was a prisoner— confined to the barge in which he travelled.

CANNON.

Speaking of cannon, the veracious traveller says: "I observed, near one of the gates of Pekin, a few rude, ill-shapen, and disproportionate pieces, lying unmounted on the ground, and these, with some of the same kind on the frontiers of Canton, and a few pieces, apparently twelve-pounders, at *Hang-choo-foo*, which had wooden pent-houses erected over each, were the only cannon that we noticed in the whole country." (p. 302.)

We presume either the fact collector, himself, or his printer, must have made a small mistake here; that instead of "we noticed" it was meant *are to be noticed.* However, Mr. Barrow happens to elucidate this subject of cannon by an engraved plate of various pieces seen in China; and it appears, from this plate, that cannon were seen at three other places besides those he has specified. In addition to this, Sir George Staunton, in the company of the F.R.S., too, saw cannon at Tinghai. Dr. Dinwiddie mentions others that were seen at two different stations along the Grand canal, and also at the entrance of the Nimpo river. So much for the only cannon.

Respecting the pieces seen at Hanchoo, Sir George Staunton, endorsing the sentiments of the ambassador, says they were two to four pounders; and Captain Parish, an officer well qualified to judge, sets them down at four pounders. Not-withstanding this authority, Mr. Barrow must let his readers know that he also was acquainted with the caliber of guns, and up they go, at once, to twelve pounders. Thus, the opinion of a qualified judge is multiplied so many times in order to reach the standard of the *Travels*. Had Captain Parish made use of a rash, and particularly an extravagant opinion, it would, no doubt, have been worth our author's attention, and probably after all improved upon; but sentiments according to reason and common sense will be either thrown aside as worthless, or *a la Barrow*, so completely disfigured as hardly to be known.

WHIMS ON PECHELEE.

The soil and population of the province of Pechelee illustrate a very remarkable whim; few more so in the whole volume. The peasantry of this ill-starred province are represented as the worst specimens of humanity seen in all China, and our author draws the most frightful caricatures of their condition, summing up his views in the quotation—

"No eye hath seen such scarecrows." (p. 553.)

Nevertheless, on the same authority, the *Travels*, when entering the adjoining province of Shantong, they were "such lank, sickly - looking, ill - clothed creatures, that the whole groupe appeared to be much fitter for an hospital than performing any kind of labor." (p. 502.) Entering the next province of Kiangnan, they "are half-starved, half-naked;" and in the next succeeding provinces "the poor wretches were in so miserable a condition, both with regard to their clothing and their habit of body," &c. (p. 531.) Similar samples from other districts can be produced also from our author, who stoutly affirms that the condition of the peasantry improved in proportion as they receded from the capital. In support of this view the "large quarto" teems with observations, or rather assertions, heaping one absurdity on to another. Never was a cause argued with less judgment or common sense. The very animus is discernible in the anxiety to carry conviction ; and after all our author's own experience proves the peasantry of the proscribed province were the *most honest, most willing, most cheerful, most able,* and *best conditioned* men that he encountered within the pale of the Chinese empire. At Ton-choo, about three thousand porters were required to carry the baggage to Pekin, and here is the fact collector's confession : " The Chinese porters showed such expedition, strength, and activity, as could not, I believe, be paralleled or procured in so short a time in any other country. Everything here, in fact, seems to be at the instant command of the state ; and the most laborious tasks are undertaken and executed with a readiness, and even a cheerfulness, which one could scarcely expect to meet with in so despotic a government." (p. 87.)

In what other province did he experience such men ? And these—his first impressions—are entirely borne out by all the other witnesses on the embassy, and particularly our private authority, quoted at page 65 of this inquiry. But the comptroller would almost persuade us he expected something superhuman on his arrival in the country, as " their general appearance was such as not to indicate any extraordinary degree of happiness or comfort." (p. 71.) *Extraordinary degree of happiness!* whoever dreamed of the like ! If they were happy, without the preposterous qualification, what more could be desired ? and so they were. The first look had scarcely shattered his expectations, when a second look convinced him— " The cheerful and good-natured countenances of the multitude were extremely prepossessing ; not less so their accommodating behaviour to one another. There was an innocence and simplicity in their features, that seemed to indicate a happy and contented turn of mind." (p. 80.)

Where, in the wide world, could he have sought for a peasantry more to be envied than this much-abused one of the province of Pechelee ? The great champion of Irish rights would scarcely have dared to enter the lists with such an opponent.(*ee*) All this, however, is merely a specimen of that detested infatuation that keeps struggling to unite, or assimilate, first impressions to future and directly opposite ones, acquired through different channels. In the first—we read our author's own experience; in the other—the experience of the Dutch embassy, which has proved a happy windfall, notwithstanding all the contempt manifested for it.

The embassy just alluded to passed through a part of Pechelee unseen by Mr. Barrow, and, in the exuberance of his views upon the doomed province, he draws the following corroborative testimony: "The farther they advanced the more miserable and poor was the apparent condition of the people, and the face of the country." (p. 208.) How unfortunate for this testimony! upon the carefully constructed map, and along the very route of the Dutch, are some of those "interesting remarks" expressive of the country being perfectly level, abounding with trees, laid out into garden grounds, and richly cultivated. By endorsing the experience of the Dutch our author sells his "interesting remarks" at a very low figure, and we are well satisfied not under their just value.

WASTE LANDS.

As agriculturists the Chinese are convicted of being total strangers to the great comprehensive systems practised in England. In consequence, they have no knowledge of improving or reclaiming waste lands, as testified by the following argument. "For want of this knowledge, a very considerable portion of the richest land, perhaps, in the whole empire, is suffered to remain a barren and unprofitable waste. If an idea may be formed from what we saw in the course of our journey, and from the accounts that have been given of the other provinces, I should conclude, that one-fourth part of the whole country nearly consists of lakes, and low, sour, swampy grounds, which are totally uncultivated." (p. 567.)

A very good field, certainly, for an enterprising farmer; but what right has the veracious traveller to assert that the richest lands of China are likely to be found in the low, sour, swampy grounds? However, as to the extent of these low, sour, swampy grounds, he entertains a very different idea when marshalling his theories in support of a redundant population. The country, then, becomes so well cultivated that he concludes—"There are no grounds for supposing the interior parts of China are deserts"—(p. 584) that is—uncultivated swamps; and yet he has just asserted that "one-fourth part of the whole country" is so. In this manner are the whims on one subject arrayed against the whims on another.

CIVILITIES TO THE EMBASSY.

The sudden dismissal of Lord McCartney from Pekin confounded the whole embassy, and upset their schemes of a winter's campaign in that capital; but, on recovering himself, Sir George Staunton struggled manfully to ward off this seeming disgrace, and his apologies, though somewhat transparent, are yet proofs of ability, and a willing mind to die a hard death. Seeing the resolute attitude of the master, it naturally occurs to the pupil to arrange himself on the same side, and, consequently, we find the following civilities scattered on his returning path.

"As a singular proof of attention shown to us in the commencement of this journey, it was observed, that whenever the chief officers of the provinces, through which the embassy was to pass, prepared an entertainment in honour of the occasion, they had given themselves all possible trouble to render it more acceptable, by endeavoring to serve it up, as they thought, in the English style. In some of these feasts we had hogs roasted whole, that could not have weighed less than fifty pounds," &c· (p. 489.)

Now, all these civilities were experienced when ascending the Pyho. The roasting of entire hogs, and the endeavors to cook and serve up in the English style, commenced with the first arrival of the embassy in the country, which the reader will find by a reference to the work of Sir George Staunton; consequently it was *not* "a singular proof of attention" on account of the return journey. But, curiously enough, upon the return journey no such entertainments were prepared by the chief officers of the provinces through which the embassy passed. The whole gist of the extract is merely the reproduction of another piece of information from the official volumes; and the dismissal, instead of the arrival, of the embassy is selected for the purpose. There is a little bit of low cunning in all this. To repeat with the master the same information in its proper place, or order, assumes too much of the copyist, and to avoid this, as far as practicable, some other occasion is sought out.(*ff.*)

Civilities of another kind are brought forward at Hanchoo, where the new viceroy of Canton was introduced to the ambassador. "He had travelled post from Pekin, and, with many assurances on the part of the emperor of the highest satisfaction he had derived from the embassy, he brought an additional present from him to his majesty, consisting of gold tissued silks, purses taken from his own person, and the *card of happiness.*"(*gg*) (p. 528.)

So far from travelling post from Pekin, with these presents, the new viceroy had not yet quitted the seat of his late government of Chekiang, and was still residing at Hanchoo, awaiting the arrival of the ambassador. In the work of Sir George Staunton this is stated, and repeated, in language impossible to be mistaken.

"As a particular mark of his imperial majesty's attention to the wishes of the English, he had made a change in the government of that province, (Canton) and named to it a person of his own blood, who was endued with uncommon sentiments of justice and benignity towards strangers ; that he had written in the strongest terms to this new viceroy, who had not yet quitted his late government of Chekiang." Sontazin also said, " As the new viceroy of Canton still resided at Hanchoo, the capital of Chekiang, he would introduce the ambassador there to him." (II, p. 414.)

The records of literature may produce contradictions of much greater importance, but certainly none more positive ; and however surprised we may be at all this, we are still more so at the tacit acknowledgment of the guardians of public opinion, one and all of which, whatever may have been the view of a particular whim, have never doubted the truthfulness of Mr. Barrow's own experience. Nothing, indeed, but the most superficial acquaintance with the " Authentic Account," joined to the most unbounded confidence in the "facts and observations," could have induced any writer to overlook assertions so audaciously contradictory to the established record : it is a disgrace to the intelligence of the age. " Reviews, in general," it has been well observed, " seem only fitted to amuse, and throw dust in the eyes of the multitude."

BARROW'S JOURNAL.—YANGTSEKIANG.

The official account of the embassy relies, not unfrequently, for assistance on Mr. Barrow, whose "journal is oftener quoted than named." On applying the proper test, however, a peculiarity escapes, not only in the language itself, but in the mode of making the extract, which leaves room to doubt if it ever belonged to any journal. For instance, the writer of the sentiments extracted is represented as speaking of himself in the third person ; while the style, even the very words, are those of the minister plenipotentiary himself. Speaking of the sources of the Yangtsekiang, we read—it " consisted" of two branches. This is the minister to a nicety ; he is far more interested in the past than in the present ; wandering among what has been, instead of what is now. But the attempts at describing the Yangtsekiang and Hohangho rivers could at best be but a subsequent addition to a journal when revised for a particular object. Whoever may have furnished the information, the paragraphs themselves, are evidently the work of the author of the "Authentic Account." But, laying all this aside for the present, let us investigate the description of the Yangtsekiang. After a southerly course of seventy miles, the two branches unite and flow to the north-east, six hundred miles ; thence eastwardly to the sea, eight hundred miles more ; and these three sums we are told, innocently enough, amount to two thousand, two hundred miles, the total length of the river from its source to the sea. (II, p. 422.) The distances are all in words, correctly spelt, and of a nature to exonerate the printer—even to preclude the idea of an accidental mistake, or seemingly anything else but reckless miscalculation. We have the authority of Sir George Staunton that Mr. Barrow made it so ; and we have the authority of Mr. Barrow, that whatever Sir George says—is right.

BRONZE LION—Engraved Representation of.

Another of these pretended quotations describes two bronze lions at Yuen-min-yuen, thus : " So totally unlike are they to what they were intended to represent, as appears by the annexed engraving of one of them, that they might almost be mistaken for knights in armour, with periwigs such as were worn in the time of King Charles." (II, p. 311.)

To have entered the above in his journal, Mr. Barrow must have had before him a copy of the official account, with the engraved figure of the lion, and, as a necessary consequence, containing the very paragraph he was then taking notes of. Sir George Staunton is also placed in the ridiculous position

of quoting an illustration which was already in his own
" splendid work." Such would be the conclusion of a hyper-
critic, and not without reason. All these pretended extracts,
in short, convey internal evidence of so many separate paragraphs, or papers, drawn up after the return of the embassy,
to assist in swelling the great compilation to its *wise-like* proportions. As already shown, they read, one and all, clearly
the offspring of Sir George Staunton, but for particular
reasons fathered, clumsily enough, upon his pupil, who, it is
evident, never kept a journal in the proper sense of the word.
His subsequent writings bear testimony against him ; and in
every instance, the official extracts are more or less inconsistent
with the *Travels*. But besides all this, we have our author's
express acknowledgment that he only took " loose notes,"
and " various and miscellaneous memoranda."

*   *   *   *   *

Turn to whatever subject we will, we thus find some mani-
festations of extravagance, some clashing whims, some reckless
blundering, or, still worse, detested inventions, ever accompanying the " unbiassed conclusions " of the great fact collector.
Whoever undertakes to explore the intricacies of the " large
quarto " enters, indeed, upon a Herculean task, where, like the
spontaneous productions of a native wilderness, every species
of iniquity thickens as he proceeds. It is by no means necessary to look about for examples: every page is teeming ; but
we have been guided in selecting some of the most prominent
to illustrate the ever-varying tints employed upon this gigantic
imposture. By far the greater number of incidents, " facts
and observations," are such that it would be idle and endless
to waste time in examining them, and these we mean to dismiss
somewhat summarily, or in groups, in the following manner :

AMUSING ANECDOTES.

The amusing anecdotes, which occasionally help to enliven
the tedium of the official volumes, would evidently not be

allowed to "waste their sweetness" on that atmosphere alone : accordingly we find them diffusing their fragrance also in the *Travels*. Belonging to this class of "pretty little dears" are the "Duke of Bedford's picture"—the "Coachman's seat on the emperor's carriage"—and the "Guards in their scarlet plumes"—all of which no doubt passed, and might have continued to pass current had not the "powerful motive" fashioned them to its own standard. No sooner, indeed, are they sent forth *a la Barrow* when their significance becomes apparent— when they assume that "questionable shape" that eventually leads to their destruction. We do not enter into particulars beyond observing that the alterations and discrepancies, not to speak of contradictions, are such that the improved version renders the original worthless, and at best to have been concocted from the most paltry considerations. Had Sir George Staunton lived he would have had little reason to thank his pupil for the "valuable addition" to his own "splendid work." These anecdotes would either have been in better keeping, or what is more likely, the world would never have been troubled with the "Travels in China:" their author, surely, could not have braved the master to his face.

But great as the discrepancies are in some of these anecdotes just named—they are even more so in that of the "Three English creating alarm in one of the strongest cities of China." Unwilling to let well-enough alone, materials are here piled on materials till the structure totters by its own weight, as testified by a simple comparison of the two accounts. Besides a tissue of contradictions from first to last, the nature of some of the statements carry the infamous stamp in their very face. For instance, Sir George Staunton, in introducing the anecdote, observes—"it happened about this time." If it happened at all, it must have happened during the three days the embassy lay before Hanchoo, and nothing could be more stupid than to say—"about this time." While this shows the baronet's caution in ignoring dates, and other definite particulars, he has absolutely committed himself while trying to avoid it.

The expression is such as could only have been used at a distant period, when writing without notes or a distinct knowledge of the affair ; or, what amounts to the same thing, concocting it. Even in that case the expression, like too many others, is stupid. But the commotion aroused in every part of the city is still more glaring : this would inevitably have reached every ear—have startled the whole embassy, and been a topic of general conversation, which was not the case. And, besides, we have the fullest assurance, from Anderson, that no remarkable event occurred during their short stay at Hanchoo. It is impossible for this journalist to have made use of such an expression had the "commotion" taken place. All the observations—recorded in our manuscript—only tend to confirm this statement ; and while destroying our belief in this—they do so in every anecdote related by Sir George Staunton, and particularly when accompanied by the "valuable" improvements of his pupil.

UNASSAILABLE INCIDENTS—Evening Entertainment.

Many of the incidental occurrences of the *Travels* are of a nature that, beyond their own suspicious dress, it would be impossible, we believe, to confute them had the *Auto* not come to our assistance. This garrulous pet seldom fails to give a version materially different from its elder brother ; and as an illustration of the credit to be reposed in even these occurrences, we produce the Evening entertainment at Canton.

As related in the prime of life, we read : " Our two worthy conductors met at Canton an old acquaintance who was governor of a city in Fokien. He gave them an evening entertainment on the river in a splendid yacht to which I was privately invited. On entering the great cabin I found the three gentlemen with each a young girl by his side very richly dressed, the cheeks, lips, and chin highly *rouged*, the rest of the face and neck whitened with a preparation of ceruse. I was welcomed by a

cup of hot wine from each of the ladies, who first sipped by
way of pledging me. During supper, which for number and
variety of dishes exceeded anything I had hitherto met with in
the country, the girls played upon the flute and sung several
airs, but there was nothing very captivating either in the vocal
or instrumental part of the music. We passed a most convivial evening free from any reserve or restraint, but on going
away, I was particularly desired by *Van* not to take any notice
of what I had seen, apprehensive, I suppose, that their brother
officers might condemn their want of prudence in admitting a
barbarian to witness this occasional relaxation from good
morals. The yacht and the ladies it seemed were hired for
the occasion." (p. 192.)

In the fulness of years the same entertainment assumes
this shape. " One evening Lee came to me with a message
from Van requesting me to return with him to his yacht to
join a small party of his friends, apologising for not sending
the usual card of invitation. I returned with Lee in his boat
to Van's yacht, and was introduced to a handsome apartment,
and severally to three elegant well-dressed ladies each of whom
I was desired to salute. Next I was presented to a third
gentleman the new governor of Canton. The ladies were
much amused at my clumsy attempts to speak their language,
but being prompted by Van to ask them to favor me with some
music and singing, they readily let me know by their compliance that they had none of that vice which Horace ascribes
to all singers, for all three struck up forthwith accompanied
by an instrument of the same nature as the guitar. The ladies
conducted themselves with great decorum, yet I felt anxious to
know who and what they were, but the question was not to be
asked; and after taking a cup of tea with some fruit and cakes
in about an hour Lee came for me in our boat. I asked him
if he knew anything of these ladies, but he said he had been
so long out of his own country that he had almost forgotten
the manners of his countrymen. He did not know whether
Van and Chou had their first or second wives in their own barges

with them; but he believed one of the three to be the wife of the governor of Canton, and the other two her friends." (p. 114.)

Now, beyond being at such a party, no two statements are alike. By the *Travels*,—the third gentleman was governor of a city in Fokien : by the *Auto*,—the new governor of Canton. By the *Travels*,—the ladies were hired for the occasion : by the *Anto*,—one was understood to be the wife of the governor of Canton, and the other two her friends. By the *Travels*,— the supper, for number and variety of dishes, exceeded anything met with in the country : by the *Auto*,—it amounted to a cup of tea, some fruit, and cakes. By the *Travels*,—the ladies sung and played upon the flute : by the *Auto*,—they sung and played upon the guitar. By the *Travels*, — the author spent a most convivial evening : by the *Auto*,—he was called away in about an hour. By the *Travels*,—he was free from all restraint : by the *Auto*,—he could not pop the question. In short, the inconsistencies of this entertainment will only cease when every comparison has been made. Here, then, is a circumstance, so far as the matter of fact is concerned, free from every attack of collateral testimony, and yet, in an instant, it is demolished by the author of it himself. If he takes such liberties with his own private matters, it may easily be conceived that the anecdotes of Sir George Staunton would not be spared. It is not a little remarkable that the last version of this affair shews a great improvement in the feelings of our author, whose disposition to indulge in subjects of lax morality and filthiness is not the least offensive part of the *Travels*, and for all of which he has never offered a good apology. Having, however, in his mellow age, destroyed this sweet production of the prime of life, it adds another to the many proofs of the disgraceful materials employed upon the " large quarto."

MYSTERIOUS ADVENTURES—Visit to Linsin Pagoda.

A very considerable proportion of the comptroller's adven

tures are presented in an unfinished state : they have either no beginning or no termination. Indeed, in some instances, both the extremes are wanting, as examplified in his visits to the pagoda at Linsin, and the cemetery at Tiensing. On these occasions he becomes manifest, the reader knows not how, or why ; and, after cutting a few dashes, he vanishes in the same mysterious manner, to become visible again, on some other occasion. We have, elsewhere, (p. 59) given good reasons for pronouncing the visit to the pagoda, now named, a scandalous imposition, but we are enabled to call in another witness to confirm it ; and, as a general illustration of mysterious mani-festations, we bring the parties face to face, allowing the culprit to speak first.

" The pagoda of *Lintsin,* an octagonal pyramid, was erected, perhaps, as a monument of this great and useful undertaking, which, however, in its present state, apparently had not stood many ages. In the hope of finding within it some inscription, that might point out its designation, we mounted with some difficulty upon the first of its nine stages or roofs, (for the little door on a level with the ground was walled up with bricks,) but it contained only the bare walls, not even a stair-case remained, nor any possible means of ascending to the top, and the lower part was choaked up with rubbish." (p. 503.)

Such are the sentiments of the comptroller on his visit to the pagoda at Linsin, but we are entirely left to conjecture how he appeared on the spot ; because he was on board his barge an hour afterwards, and there was no stoppage to render such a visit possible. However, we introduce a witness whose visit labors under no difficulty, and who examined and described this pagoda in a manner consistent with human comprehension.

" At the nearest angle of the bank some others and myself landed, and found no difficulty in entering and ascending to the top of the building. It is of an octagonal form of nine stories diminishing to the summit : the foundation and nearly the whole of the first story are of stone or porphoritic granite, the remainder is of brick glazed on the surface. Four Chinese

words are inscribed on the outside signifying the relics of Fo:
the building is, therefore, a temple to that god and is called
Shayli Pata. We ascended by a winding staircase of one
hundred and eighty-three steps—the steps and curves of the
walls are of porphoritic granite highly polished. There are
several slabs of the same stone, which by some has been called
marble. The glazed bricks have been also described as porce-
laine. With the exception of the landing place the building is
in good repair, and is certainly an interesting specimen of this
style of architecture. The roof of the story projects nearly two
feet and is highly decorated with carved work. The whole is
covered in with cast-iron or bell metal. I estimated the height
at one hundred and forty feet. We had a good view of the
city of Linsin from the top. There are so many gardens within
the walls that no buildings are to be distinguished. A miao,
near the pagoda, with a gilt colossal idol, would, unless eclipsed
by its neighbor, deserve a visit. There are two idols in the
Pagoda itself—one on the first, the other on the highest story :
the latter is of baked clay. The walls of the city, seen from
the top, appeared about two miles distant."

Who, after this, could hesitate to pronounce the Barrow-
visit a bare-faced forgery. Unless in the character of the
architecture, and the number of its stories—to ascertain which
it was not necessary to land—every other feature is inconsistent with the straightforward description. Covering with a
veil the *deplorable rubbish* which the comptroller has thrown
inside the building, we find his ignorance of the outside, itself,
only what could have been expected from a passing gaze, at a
distance. Neither the porphoritic basement, nor the glazed
bricks, nor the carved roof, he pretends to have scaled with
difficulty, arrested his attention : nay! more — the very
"inscription" he was in search of! *Shayli Pata*, was there,
staring him in the very face, and yet, alas! Mr. Barrow, with
all the liberty he enjoyed, and with all the language he had
acquired, collected not this "fact." Truly, it was "the lot
of few to go to Pekin!" but though our favored traveller

knew this, he did not perceive he was, ere long, to be
followed by one who would expose such shameless impositions.
If the author of the *Travels* possessed a spark of contrition, it
must have pricked his conscience on reading the journal of
Mr. Ellis, even after the healing virtues of the Quarterly had
been poured out in mitigation of the pain. We wonder if it
ever occurred to Mr. Barrow, as a reviewer, to try his pen
upon his own *Travels*; or those of his amiable patron : we are
well assured that great fault would be found with the works of
other writers who *infinitely* less deserved it. (*hh*)

PALATIAL INCIDENTS—Emperor's favorite Draughtsman.

The numerous incidents said to have transpired at the palace
of Yuen-min-yuen rank among the most difficult to rebut by
external testimony. In no one instance is the subject twice
mentioned, and the only person who could be supposed to throw
any light thereon is entirely silent; but even this silence is
not without its meaning, as the following instance will testify.
According to the comptroller, the emperor sends his favorite
draughtsman to Yuen-min-yuen, to make drawings of the
principal presents to carry to his master, in Tartary, as eluci-
dations of the descriptive catalogue. "Every part of the
machines, except the naked figures which supported the time-
piece and a barometer, he drew with neatness and accuracy,
but all his attempts to copy these were unsuccessful. Whether
it was owing to any real difficulty that exists in the nice turns
and proportions of the human figure, or that by being better
acquainted with it we more readily perceive the defects in the
imitation of it, or from the circumstance of the human form
being concealed in this country in loose folding robes, that
caused the Chinese draughtsman so completely to fail, I leave
to the artists of our own country to determine : but the fact
was as I state it; all his attempts to draw these figures were
preposterous."   (p. 326.)

Attention has already been drawn to the suspicious dress in which the collector of facts clothes his elucidating incidents. The draughtsman must, in consequence, be the emperor's *favorite*: if he could not draw it would be idle to look for one that could. This dignified personage, however, is totally unknown to Dr. Dinwiddie, who was more interested in these machines than any other person; and who was not even a single hour absent from the palace for the space of three weeks, during the first of which the draughtsman must have been at the work that was to elucidate the descriptive catalogue. Eunuchs, princes, mandarines, private citizens, French, Italian, and Portuguese missionaries, the gentlemen of the mathematical tribunal, and even gentlemen of the English embassy—all are noticed at the palace, but not a word of this favorite draughtsman, than whom none was more likely to have drawn the doctor's attention. But, what is still more extraordinary, we are informed that Mr. Alexander, the draughtsman to the embassy, came to the palace and took sketches of the principal machines; and these sketches were carried into Tartary along with the descriptive catalogue. The circumstance of the English draughtsman, then, smacks strongly of having given the hint by which our author might introduce a piece of information previously detailed in the official volumes. When at Gehol, Sir George Staunton took notice of some pictures in which the artist failed to draw the human figure, though able in other respects; and this information is exactly reproduced by the incident of the "Favorite draughtsman." The particular circumstance—which caused this draughtsman "so completely to fail"—Mr. Barrow leaves to the decision of English artists, and we are perfectly satisfied to follow the example.

At Gehol, too, in the emperor's villa, were certain works of art which the legate asserted to be the productions of China, but was answered by the gentlemen who informed him that the works in question came from England. Exactly in a similar manner, the comptroller, at Yuen-min-yuen, discovers some

pictures to have been executed by an Italian, named Castagli-
one, although the old eunuch endeavored to persuade him (our
author) that they were the work of Chinese artists. Even a
musical clock, with the name of Clarke, Leadenhall Street,
was asserted, by the same capricious old gentleman, to be a
piece of Chinese mechanism. Such are specimens of the
palatial anecdotes, which are numerous, and, had they been
true, interesting ; but we now leave them, observing only that
in nearly every instance a prototype can be produced.

INVESTIGATION CONTINUED.

BARROW *versus* STAUNTON.

OFFICIAL VOLUMES.

Hitherto, we have been chiefly interested in the cause of
Barrow *versus* Barrow, with only occasional allusions to that of
Barrow *versus* Staunton, a matter of equal importance, and
which demands some further examination. The official narrative of the embassy is always mentioned in flattering terms.
It is the "Authentic Account;" the "valuable work;" to
sum up, "It would be an idle, and, indeed, a superfluous
undertaking, in any other person who accompanied the embassy,
to dwell on those subjects which have been treated by him in
so masterly a manner; or to recapitulate those incidents and
transactions, which he has detailed with equal elegance and
accuracy." (p. 1.) By the *Auto*, our author even assumes no
small merit in this matchless compilation: he is, in some
measure, a junior editor, or co-partner in the concern. Notwithstanding his connexion with the work; and notwithstanding
the praise he has bestowed upon it, he, the comptroller, has
undertaken to *recapitulate*, and to *correct* the very incidents he
holds up to the mirror as specimens of "elegance and accuracy"
He has, in fine, written not only in violation of the work itself,
but in violation of his own sentiments of that work. It would
be idle to expect the name of Sir George Staunton associated

with even the smallest oversight; the very thought would be too bare-faced an insult to the author of so much good fortune. Correct *ad libitum*, mangle and disfigure as it may seem proper, but keep the name of the amiable and liberal gentleman out of sight—rather, if possible, point in an opposite direction. This is the principle upon which the submissive pupil sets to work, and, of course, a single statement is never called in question—*directly*. That it has been done so—*indirectly*—we have already given proof, and shall now confirm it by the amplest evidence. Before proceeding further, however, we have to observe that ignoring a matter of fact by the introduction of another is tantamount to a denial of the former.

KEETO WHIRLPOOL.

When the squadron anchored off Chusan, the Clarence brig, with Sir George Staunton and Mr. Barrow aboard, was dispatched thither to procure pilots. The whole history of this short expedition is a texture of outrageous contradictions, against which the patience of Job would not suffice. It is not merely discrepancies arising from difference of opinion, or defective memory, but the clashing of facts, which the ablest advocacy of sophism can never reconcile. In the dusk of the evening, according to the official account, they approached the projecting promontary called Keeto. " Round this point the tide ran in whirling eddies, with a rapidity that would force into its vortex a ship of the largest size, unless a strong breeze enabled her to sail past it. Within a hundred yards of the point, the mud is brought up from the bottom in such quantities as to excite alarm, least the ship should strike the ground, in those who are not aware of the vast depth of water in this spot, which exceeds one hundred fathoms. A little to the southward of the point the Clarence found good anchorage, in seventeen fathoms, where it was thought prudent to remain that night." With the early morning tide, accompanied by a

Chinese junk, she proceeded into the harbour of Chusan. (I, p. 413.)

It is impossible to mistake the language just quoted—that the brig anchored to the south of Keeto, where it was deemed prudent to remain for the night, rather than encounter the peculiarities of the point, at such an hour. Ignoring this anchorage, however, and the reasons for it, Mr. Barrow writes "As we approached, in the Clarence brig, the high rocky point of the continent called *Keeto*, which juts into the midst of the cluster of islands, the wind suddenly failed us ; and the current hurried us with such velocity directly towards the point, that we expected momentarily to be dashed to pieces." His protecting deity, however, reserved him for a *better fate.* " On coming within twice the length of the ship of the perpendicular precipice, which was some hundred feet high, the eddy swept her round three several times with great rapidity," the last whirl sending her into a smooth uniform current, along with which she moved rapidly on the voyage, till stopped and brought to anchor by a Chinese junk. (p. 53.)

Both accounts are not true. The brig did not both *pass* and *not pass* the point that evening, and the obligations of truth demanded from Mr. Barrow an explanation of this manifest impossibility. The details of the official account were acknowledged to be " elegant and accurate," and as such had been established for years ; yet, in an instant, an attempt is made to smash them without any reason being assigned, or even an allusion made to them. Singularly enough, the would-be smasher, himself, has furnished the means of setting the difficulty at rest. The track of the Clarence, on this occasion, is laid down upon the chart of the Chusan islands, and the spot where she anchored pointed out, according to Sir George Staunton, and in direct violation of Mr. Barrow, who claims to be the author of the chart.

Again : on the return voyage, four days afterwards, Sir George Staunton acquaints us the Clarence passed close to Sarah Galley island, where, "the wind dying away, she drifted into an eddy, in which she was whirled round, as upon a centre, several times, with much impetuosity. At every revolution the bowsprit was within a few feet of striking against a steep rock that rose perpendicularly out of the sea." (I, p. 436.)

Here are all the main features of the former occasion repeated four days afterwards, close to an island, opposite, and at least two miles from the promontary. Respecting this outward occurrence—the *Travels* are as mute as the grave. All this smacks of a disgraceful imposition somewhere : one author—ignoring the terrific encounter at Keeto point, but giving good reasons for it ; the other author—ignoring the second encounter off Sarah Galley, without any reason whatever. As Mr. Barrow has committed himself on the anchorage, it is easy to see upon whose shoulders the responsibility of the imposition lies. In short, it is beyond the possibility of a doubt that the occurrence off Sarah Galley Island has been reproduced, " according to the custom of the manor," which shifts the particulars as far as time and situation admits. When steering clear of his patron—the man in search of facts knew there was greater scope for embellishment, and hence the anecdote of the priest and sailor. Magnificent facts ! O England ! how fortunate was thy lot in selecting at least one right man for the right place !

With an assurance that is truly lamentable, the *Auto* endorses the encounter off Keeto point, which both Sir George Staunton and the chart prove to be an impudent invention ; it even adds to the infamy by endeavoring to give a color for the return occasion, which was the only eddy the brig whirled in. It is lamentable, we repeat, to find the hoary sinner heaping the coals about his own head when he should have been attending to his quietus.(*ii*)

It is even significant that the " Lion " and " Hindostan," while working their way to and from Chusan harbor, found nothing worthy of their logs arising from the " tumultuous eddies, boiling around Keeto point," and to paint which the disciple of truth had to draw so largely on the Messinian fraternity. He relies greatly for aid on such comparisons, or on a poetic distich, aids which truth never require, but without which romance would languish for want of food till it assumed the appearance of the " half-naked, half-starved wretches" that so reluctantly dragged him through the scenes of his *Travels*.

CHOLERA MORBUS.

Another circumstance, quite as irreconcileable, is thus introduced by Sir George Staunton. "During the stay of the Clarence in Chusan harbor, one of the persons who came in her was seized with a violent cholera morbus, in consequence of eating too freely of some acid fruit he had found on shore." Inquiries were immediately made for a Chinese physician; such a physician *soon* arrived and relieved the patient. (I, p. 435.)

Whenever Sir George Staunton alludes to a gentleman in connexion with any particular transaction or occurrence, without mentioning the party by name, Mr. Barrow almost always steps in as the hero of the occasion; and in consequence we find him cutting the most conspicuous figure throughout the whole embassy. For this reason, we are not at all surprised to find him laying claims to have been the victim of the cholera morbus; but with what credibility our readers shall have an opportunity of judging. By the language of Sir George Staunton, it is very clear that the party, whoever it was, had found the fruit on shore. Nevertheless, the willing victim assures us the sickness arose from eating " sea blubber," or fruit, while at anchor off Keeto point, upwards of ten miles from the harbor, and at least thirty hours before one of the gentlemen had been ashore. (p. 55.) It was then not only dark, but an intricate channel rendered the *immediate* arrival of a physician an impossibility, and particularly one sent by the governor, who, according to our author, had reported himself in a distant part of the island. On another page of the *Travels* (345) their wise author does acknowledge the sickness to have occurred at Chusan, from " eating too freely of unripe fruit"— not a word of the " sea blubber." But occur where, or how, it is, with the *Travels*, "a severe sickness for several days," although Sir George Staunton says the patient was *soon* relieved. By bringing in another witness, the *Auto*, the governor's physician changes into a venerable gentleman practising in the city of Tinghai, and who made Mr. Barrow " himself again after twenty-four hours of severe suffering." (p. 62.)

We shall not make an effort to pluck a single well-earned leaf from the laurel which adorns the brow of Mr. Barrow ; neither shall we flinch a step to protect those that are unmerited. Amidst all this rubbish, a few facts are discovered sufficient to set the matter at rest. The brig lay a whole day and part of two others in the harbor ; and during the last two days only were the gentlemen on shore. The first of these two days was entirely spent on shore, and the evening considerably advanced before the party got on board. If Mr. Barrow, then, was seized with cholera morbus it must have been in the night time, or on the following morning ; but, instead of twisting and writhing in the agonies of death, he is again early ashore, attending to the business of the pilots, who are " the most miserable wretches he ever beheld." If he was the victim, the pilots have been shamefully traduced : if he was not the victim, he has shamefully disgraced himself. From either point of view the " facts" are presented in their true colours—they are *disgusting*. Like all other occurrences, this of the cholera morbus has been turned to good account, furnishing as it does a perfect illumination on the native practice of medicine.

The more we inquire into this Chusan expedition, the more we are convinced of the wisdom of the adage, " Liars should have good memories." This adage, however, seems exemplified in our author in a sense not usually understood. That he possessed an excellent memory is fully borne out by the pertinent use he makes of all authors, ancient and modern; while the reckless contradiction of himself, and of the patron for whom he stands sponsor, is conclusive of the second part of the premises. He was, in short, a liar, and had a good memory.

VISIT TO TINGHAI.

The visit which the gentlemen made to the town of Tinghai is no less teeming with inconsistencies. By the official account, they travelled well over the place, and were much interested : by the non-official—the heat and crowd were so great that before they had travelled *one* street they took shelter in a temple, from which they returned in sedan chairs, rather disappointed than gratified. Indeed, such was the popular feeling, "that the bearers were stopped every moment by the crowd, in order that every one might satisfy his curiosity by thrusting his head in at the window, and exclaiming, with a grin, *Hungmau! Englishman*, or literally, *Redpate!*" (p. 57.) Ignoring this extraordinary impert- inence, the official narrative informs us, "They were familiar, but without insult, scoff, or uproar." While con- firming the shelter in the temple, the last authority, again, ignores the civilities received there, as mentioned by the comptroller; but, on the other hand, admits similar civilities at a monastery, near the sea side, where, on their return, they also took shelter from heavy rains and violent winds that nearly upset the chairs. (I, p. 426.) This last circumstance Mr. Barrow ignores *in toto*. Now, a moment's reflection shows something supremely ridiculous in all this : one gentleman—ignoring the extraordinary liberty of being stopped every moment to be laughed at ; the other—ignoring the violent winds that nearly upset his chair, and drove him into a monastery.

CHINESE PILOTS.

Such are some of the abominations attending this visit to
Chusan, and, surprisingly enough, they never cease throughout
the whole narrative of the *Travels*. Every now and then, the
"powerful motive" is determined to manufacture something
new or strange at any cost. Respecting the two pilots procured at Chusan—Sir George Staunton says—"Each brought
with him a small marine compass." (I, p. 439.) This the
pupil confutes, at once, by asserting that " one of them, in fact,
had come on board without his compass"—(p. 61.)—the most
unlikely thing imaginable. The pilots were directed to pre-
pare themselves, and if the compass was necessary to their
duties, neither the one nor the other could have forgot it, nor
have come aboard without it. But granting it to have been
overlooked for a moment, the one with the compass must
have reminded the other. The truth evidently lies in the
combination of whims, and what not, that have given rise to
the "Travels in China." The scientific author of these
Travels, with certain theories in his head respecting the merits
of the Chinese and European instruments, may possibly have
seen one of the pilots curious, or even puzzled in the matter,
and in order to squeeze a little capital out of it, the pilot is
made to forget his compass. Altogether, the observations on
the Chinese pilots deserve the severest reprehension, and if a
flat denial were given to every statement that stands alone,
the truth would not be overstepped. They could not possibly
have shown greater ignorance of the coast than their disprover
has done in his attempts at narrative, which becomes so contemptible, and so opposed to the truth, that we wonder how
even he, with all his vanity, had the assurance of concocting
and offering such trash to the public. Through a series of
untraceable and unintelligible manœuvres, the squadron is
brought finally to anchor, and the embassy within the Chinese
territory, where, for a little, we shall bring him face to face
once more with his patron.

FIRST IMPRESSIONS—"The Unkindest Cut."

In their early progress up the Pyho, Sir George Staunton, praising the face of the country, and the appearance of the people, observes—" A general sentiment prevailed, that it was well worth while to have travelled to such a distance to behold a country which promised so interesting in every respect." (II, p. 17.)

In the face of such an acknowledgment the ungrateful pupil hurls his dissent thus : " I am persuaded every individual of the embassy felt himself rather disappointed in the expectations he had formed." (p. 71.) In plain English, Mr. Barrow is *persuaded* his amiable patron is not speaking the truth. This, indeed, seems the " unkindest cut of all." That Sir George, however, spoke his real sentiments is corroborated by every other testimony before the public ; and our private authority, speaking of the prospect from the boat, says—" The curvilineal meanderings of the river are most enchanting." Again—" The vast attention paid us by all ranks is extremely flattering." If the gentlemen really felt a disappointment—it must have been in a sense entirely opposite to what the author of the *Travels* insinuates, as their expectations, so far as can be ascertained, seem to have been more than realized. That the first impressions of the comptroller squared with the rest of the suite is beyond doubt ; but after years produced a woful change of sentiment on the northern province, and the com-piler of detestable prejudices now struggles to shape his views accordingly.

COUNTRY ON THE PYHO—Flat or not Flat.

The country through which the Pyho meanders is so flat and uniform, that Sir George Staunton is thus particular.—" Nor was there a hillock on any side between them and the horizon, until the fourth day of their departure from Tiensing, when some high blue mountains were seen rising from the north west." (II, p. 78.)

Regardless, as usual, of the " elegant and accurate" details, the lynx-eyed Mr. Barrow writes "The surface of the country, in fact, began to assume a less uniform appearance, being now partly broken into hill and dale ; but nothing approaching to a mountain was yet visible in any direction." (p. 83.)

Just before these blue mountains appeared then, the undutiful pupil is positive the surface of the country was broken into hill and dale, in direct opposition to his amiable master, who is equally positive not a hillock had been seen. The case for the former is bad indeed : his own *Travels*, and his own map, in several instances, confirm how perfectly "flat and uniform" was the country on both sides of the Pyho, even from Pekin southwards to Tonchang, a distance exceeding two hundred miles. Whenever there is an opportunity of testing these discrepancies, we always find the greater amount of probability or consistency arranged on the official side ; and, in comparison of himself, the author of the *Travels* had good reasons for admitting the details to possess " elegance and accuracy." If such discrepancies, however, might occasionally occur with honest but careless journalists, there was no excuse in the present case. Whether flat or not the fact was ascertained, and gazing in our author's eyes ; and nothing short of the wrongheadedness of insanity would induce any other man to impose such ravings on the public, as " facts and observations."

SOIL AROUND PEKIN—Rich or Sterile.

Another contrast and we have done with confronting the two " able historians" of the McCartney embassy. We allude to the soil of this extensive plain, and more particularly to that portion of it approaching to, and surrounding the Chinese capital. As he started into Tartary, the minister writes— " The soil adjoining to this flat road was like that on the other

side of Pekin, a rich loam highly cultivated." (II, p. 169.)
On another occasion it is—"A fertile country, full of culture
and villages." (II, p. 354.)

Fertile or not, the pupil affirms "The great road to the
capital lay across an open country, sandy and ill-cultivated."
(p. 91.) Also, "the very sterile and unproductive state of
the country for many miles around Pekin." (548.)

Is it likely the two authors would estimate thus from the
same data? or rather is it not evidence of imposition somewhere? It was, at all events, incumbent upon the last writer
to have assigned some reason for writing so diametrically
opposite to the "elegant and accurate" details. Had he not
stood sponsor for those details he would have saved himself
from part of the absurdities now pressing upon his own
shoulders; but, if that load were removed, he stands convicted,
even in this case, by the "interesting remarks" upon that
map which exhibits a "faithful picture of the country." Unlike the official account, too, the *Travels* labor under that
woful change which subsequently fell like a thunderclap on the
soil and peasantry surrounding the capital.

* * * * * * * *

These specimens, while furnishing a clear insight into the
Barrow-mode of "book dressing," prove, satisfactorily, so far
as he is concerned that the task of re-capitulating has been a
very idle one. They also prove how empty are the servile
flourishes which he endeavors to weave round the name of the
author of his good fortune. While professing the greatest
esteem for the labors of that gentleman, he confutes and con-
tradicts, mangles and disfigures, in every variety of form, the
very sentiments he is praising for "elegance and accuracy."
As steady, however, to his text as the needle to the pole, he
never once links the honored name to the subject in question,
nor associates the sentiments with the most trifling oversight,
or difference of opinion, which must often, and necessarily,

K

occur among honest men.   No, indeed! the most outrageous
contradictions involve neither error nor difference of opinion!
Let the master detail any event with the most perfect " elegance
and accuracy," and the pupil will confute those details without
destroying their attributes! they will still be " elegant and
accurate!"   Incomprehensible as this feat may appear, the
spectators are nevertheless so carried away by the manner of
the attempt that they pour forth their plaudits before making
sure that the feat is actually accomplished.   Such is one of the
most daring improvements of the school, and such the manner
of its reception.

BARROW *versus* THE OFFICIAL MAPS.

GEOGRAPHICAL AND STATISTICAL CONTRADICTIONS.

The maps and charts, upon which the various routes of the embassy are laid down, also require a little further examination. They are in the folio volume accompanying the quarto edition of the official account, and Sir George Staunton assures us they were carefully constructed by Mr. Barrow, whose name is prefixed to the work. Notwithstanding this authority, we often find in the "large quarto" information totally at variance with, and as if such maps had never existed. A number of very remarkable instances have already been pointed out, in addition to which the following are added.

"The greatest depth of the Yellow sea, in the track of the ships, did not exceed thirty-six fathoms, and it was frequently diminished to ten fathoms." (p. 63.) But what is the fact? The charts show the depth frequently reached forty-two fathoms, and never fell so low as ten, except in one instance, when the Hindostan only deviated near the shore.

Again: "The deepest part of the wide gulf of *Pechelee* exceeds not twelve fathoms, and the prodigious number of small sandy islands, just appearing above the surface, are said to have been created within the records of history." (p. 491.)

Thus, without any other experience but the solitary soundings of the squadron, the depth of the wide gulf of Pechelee is limited to twelve fathoms. But even in the track of the ships it was frequently found more: in one spot as much as seventeen fathoms.

As to the "prodigious number of small sandy islands"— Mr. Barrow had no authority for them. None were seen in the track of the ships ; nor does the chart point to a single instance, except those at the bar where the ships finally anchored.   This example, in connexion with the preceding ones, furnishes a clear and rather beautiful insight into the operations of the " powerful motive" when collecting facts. Having made certain calculations when the mud of the Yellow river will change the Yellow sea into dry land—the owner of the " motive" is pushing on the work as fast as he can ; hence the *shallowness* of the Yellow sea, and the *prodigious* number of small sandy islands to support his calculations.

On the return route of the embassy, we are informed, " Fahrenheit's thermometer on the 14th, 15th, and 16th October stood at 52° and 53° in the morning." (p. 500.) The map, however, says 47°.

About a fortnight afterwards, in the province of Shantong, " The great extent of water had a sensible effect on the temperature of the air, especially in the mornings and evenings, when Fahrenheit's thermometer was sometimes below 40°." (p. 507.)

By the map it was never less than 45°, and that only one day.   These trifles are all in the Barrow style, and not the result of oversight or carelessness : they are purposely arranged to assist the particular whim for which they are brought forward.

" The length of that part of the canal which lies between the *Euho* and the Yellow river, and which we had now sailed over, is about two hundred English miles." (p. 511.)

Measured upon the map, the distance is over three hundred English miles, and about right, if any reliance is to be placed upon other maps.   The estimate, by the extract, is copied without acknowledgment, from Lord McCartney's journal, the merits of which have been carefully ransacked for reproduction in the *Travels*.   Several other inaccuracies have been thus repeated ; all adding their mite to elucidate the foundations of the " unbiassed conclusions."(*jj*)

" The hills along this southern coast of the gulf of Pechelee

have a very peculiar character." (p. 64.)   These hills, styled
by the gentlemen of the embassy " Mandarine's Bonnets,"
were seen along the coast of Shantong promontary several days
before the vessels entered the gulf of Pechelee.   The map
shows this, and the chief witnesses, including the culprit,
confirm it.   The hills, therefore, in reality, and also as understood at the time, did not lie on the south coast of the gulf of
Pechelee, along which the squadron never sailed.   It is headstrong stupidity, and not the only instance either originating
with these hills.   In the index, we read—" Hills of Pechelee—
character of."   As shown, the hills are neither in the province
of Pechelee, nor in the gulf of Pechelee; but in the province
of Shantong, to the east of the bay of Kisansu, rendered
memorable as the place where the pilots committed their
unpardonable blunder of mistaking one bay for another.(*kk*)

While ascending the Chentang river, "One city only
occurred in the course of seven days." (p. 529.)   Yet during
these seven days upon the map are placed no fewer than two
cities of the first class, and five cities of the third class,
independent of a note confirming the banks to be crowded
with villages.

The "powerful motive" operates in any direction, "just as
the twig is bent."   While seeing what was impossible to be
seen, the same wonderful faculty could also remain in ignorance
of the very facts that were staring in its eyes.   It is not a
little remarkable that both Lord McCartney and Sir George
Staunton take no notice of these cities, excepting one which
the baronet appears to see in a dream: they, however, only
ignore what Mr. Barrow positively denies, the very existence
of such places.   " One city *only* occurred in the course of
seven days," and that was of the third rank, at the end of the
river navigation.(*ll*)   This truly is journalising! but it is
only a fair sample of the *Travels*.   What, indeed, must have
been our notions of the interior of China had it depended upon
such authority!   Besides the map, it is proved by Anderson,
by the Dutch, and by still later travellers, that six or seven

walled cities did occur, and some of them of great commercial importance. Had one or other of them, however, been famous in the missionary records for some filthy or immoral habits, it would have been seen and speculated on, even at the distance of twenty miles. But all this only adds weight in confirmation of the trashy nature of the narrative ; and is equally conclusive of the hardihood with which the " facts and observations" are hazarded.

" The city of *Nanchangfoo* is situated upon the left bank of the *Kankiangho*." (p. 534.) In the carefully constructed map, this city is placed on the right bank, where it ought to be.

The geographical positions of the different provinces through which the embassy travelled, as described in the " large quarto," is not only opposed to the map—but would be disgraceful to the understanding of the merest schoolboy. Scarcely one of these ancient divisions is assigned to its proper place, while the blundering stupidity attending some is enough to create astonishment, had we not now ceased to be astonished at anything issuing from such a source. For instance, the provinces of Chekiang and Kiangnan, on their northern limits, are made to reach the same parallel of latitude, although the latter province lies all along, and stretches from the northern boundary of the former, at least four degrees, still further north. (p, 571-3.) The two provinces are made to occupy the same position, something in the manner of the swamp which was thrust down upon lake Cining. The parallels of Kiangsee, too, are fixed from 28° to 30°, notwithstanding, on its southern limit, this province begins at something like 24½° (p. 574.) Truth is thus mangled by the " powerful motive," even when the spotless virtue does not stand in its way. Taking into consideration the " rivers of note," and other learned " endeavors," we are compelled to admit that the geographical knowledge furnished by the *uncommon lot*, and the English syntax employed in scattering that knowledge, are exactly on a par : " equal elegance and accuracy" shining conspicuously in both.

BLUNDERING IN DATES.

In dates, too, we find many blunders, all of which along the route of the embassy look exceedingly awkward when reference is made to the map ; and it is to such only that we now draw attention. If truth had been the object of the " large quarto," and if the " loose notes" were dateless, which is likely, a glance at the map would have rendered invaluable assistance. The man, indeed, who disregards such trifles, particularly when they are within reach, will not be very nice in matters of greater importance.

By the " large quarto," the squadron is made to pass through the strait of Formosa in the month of July, when the chart, confirming the established fact, shows it was in June. (p. 34.) This is a most glaring blunder in the first edition, and still more so in the second. While it shows how very superficially the work has been read, even by reviewers, it proves our author had no intention to correct the mishaps of the " motive," which consequently are approved of.

The embassy, on its return, is made to enter the province of Shantong October 19th, when the map, again right, was ready to remind the " motive " it was on the previous day. (p. 502.)

Approaching the Shepatan, or Eighteen Cataracts, the " large quarto" substitutes the 3rd November, for the 3rd December, as shown on the map. (p. 536.)

Once more : " On the 10th (meaning it is presumed the 10th of December) we halted before a village which was just within sight of the suburbs of Canton." Here another conflict occurs with truth and the map, which point to the 19th December.(mm) (p. 600.)

As the blunders specified in the above dates are worthless, even in assisting the " powerful motive," they are evidently the result of gross carelessness in the first edition ; but having, with all other disgraceful fraternities, been copied into the second edition, they are there, with their author's consent, a lasting monument to confirm his disregard of truth. These

blunders had escaped the critics, and—confiding in the happy
ignorance of his readers—he deemed it better for them to
remain so than he—an author of "growing reputation"—
should tarnish that reputation by acknowledging his liability to
any mistake whatever. We have every confidence in this
explanation from the fact that a solitary trifling contradiction,
and a solitary low word, each pointed out by a separate review,
in the first edition, were corrected in the second; but nothing
more, unless making bad worse.

On the subject of dates, we take the opportunity of mentioning that the *Auto*, which, in its turn, is occasionally at
loggerheads with the *Travels*, has a most extraordinary blunder
of this nature; and we extract it for the benefit of our readers,
although carrying us to another forest of iniquities we have no
desire to explore. Upon one page, (140) this pet production
informs us its author landed in Cape Town, 4th May, 1797;
and, upon another page, (210) that he traversed every part of
the Cape colony between the 1st July, 1796, and 18th January,
1797. As a matter of consequence, he traversed every part
of the colony before he set foot in it. Whatever the reader
may think of this performance it is, nevertheless, quite as true
as the adventures in the Chinese empire.(*nn*)

BUNGLING.

Such of our readers as feel interested in pure bungling are
requested to compare the map with pages 607-8 of the *Travels*,
where they will find something to reward their trouble. In
the true spirit of instruction, our author undertakes to estimate
the number of men, vessels, horses, &c. that were employed in
transporting the embassy, but, whether through fatigue, or
losing himself in one of his own mists, or what,—when about
half way, the whole of the remaining part of the journey is
jumbled together to turn up as it best may. Consequently,
we find one stage repeated after being included in that which

immediately precedes it; and while the embassy is carried forward by water, it is also carried forward by land. Another stage slips through his fingers, and is never seen nor heard of afterwards. A third also disappears by assuming a new character, and getting into company with two others of an opposite affinity. From lake Poyang to Canton is set down as one stage, and the whole of it accounted for on the principle of water carriage, notwithstanding Mount Melin stands in the way. The embassy is thus transported over the mountain in vessels,—a mode of navigation which certainly does no discredit to the *Travels*.

LORD McCARTNEY'S JOURNAL.

The journal of Lord McCartney has already been alluded to as having been improperly dealt with, and we offer a few brief observations in support of this assumption. The number of suspicious entries is considerable, but we notice only those, to the subject of which attention has been drawn in this inquiry.

The first is respecting Parker's lens. It is copied and commented on, at pages 35 and 38, where our reasons are given why we think it was never written by his lordship.

Another entry, relating to the boat sticking fast in the mud of the Pyho, is also with our comments to be found at page 68. It seems perfectly incredible that his lordship should notice an occurrence which is rendered all but impossible by a host of other testimony, while it is, in a great measure, contradicted by the admissions of Mr. Barrow, himself. His lordship is made to observe that the gentlemen separated into smaller boats, and divided the baggage : but, on investigating the works of Mr. Barrow, and others, we find the gentlemen did not separate.

A third entry observes : " October 27. The canal is now conducted over a great morass which appears without limits on either side." The accounts of other writers confirm that such a swamp was never seen along the route of the embassy. On the Grand canal, at this juncture, a chain of mountains bounded the prospect on either side : those to the east highly picturesque, and at no great distance. But we refer our readers to the jottings on this day, at page 85, and leave them to their own inference.

A fourth entry reads : "Nov. 24. Last night we continued our voyage but so dense a vapor had risen in consequence of the late rains and overspread the atmosphere, that though the river widened and deepened considerably, our navigation seemed often attended with danger. Our vessels frequently struck upon the shelves, and sometimes ran foul of each other with a sudden crash; thus contributing not a little to the dismal character of the night, which was still, moist, cold, and comfortless. The mist grew every moment darker and heavier and so magnified the objects around us, that no wonder our senses and imaginations were equally deceived and disturbed, and that the temples, turrets, and pagodas, appeared to us through the fog, as we sailed along, like so many phantoms of giants and monsters flitting away from us, and vanishing in the gloom."

We are well assured that Lord McCartney could write sense, and we are equally assured that the above description destroys itself by its own insanity. We should, indeed, have strong doubts of the sanity of that individual who, on investigating the entry, and the circumstances that gave rise to it, could come to any other conclusion. The miraculous powers of the comptroller's eyes are here transferred to his lordship, who, all of a sudden, acquires the gift of distinguishing the distant temples, turrets, and pagodas, in a dismal midnight fog, that prevented one junk from steering clear of another. It is, be it remembered, at this juncture that Mr. Barrow, after swelling the river to an " enormous size," has upset one of those junks upon a rice mill ; nevertheless his lordship shuts his gifted eyes to this event. What ! then, are we to think of the feelings of a man whose attention could be drawn to the phantoms of giants and monsters flitting in the mist, or even to the crashing of the junks, and yet remain unmoved at the upsetting of one of those junks, hurling gentlemen of his train to the mercy of a raging element, at this unseemly hour. We are fully persuaded he could not be otherwise than unmoved at an event which, to a demonstration, is rendered impossible by the

united testimony of every individual who has written on the
embassy.   We are equally persuaded that the entry, though
cloaked with his lordship's name, never issued from his pen.
Instead of common sense, it betrays a delight in whimsical
extravagance, and the long hobbling periods so peculiar to the
style of the distinguished F.R.S., under whose protection it was
introduced to the world.

Another, and the last entry we shall notice, presents one
very remarkable feature.   "To the southward of Nanchoofou
the people seem less civilized than on the other side of the
mountain."

Here, we have his lordship committing an anachronism: he
describes his sensations of the behaviour of the people to the
southward of Nanyang before he, himself, had been to the
southward of that city.   The entry is made on the very day
of his arrival, and he did not start southward till after breakfast
the following morning.   That his lordship, at some subsequent
period, might have revised his journal, and made an allusion
to the ill-bred peasantry, is quite possible; but it is not
possible he could have made the entry in question; because it
is the impressions of the moment, which could not have been
written before the moment arrived; and if written afterwards
it could not have represented the uncertainty it does, when all
cause of uncertainty had been removed.   But we are assured,
by his biographer, that Lord McCartney never interfered with
his journal after the impressions of the moment.   The entry
proves that some one has interfered; and, if further evidence
were necessary, we find, on a close examination, that the two
insignificant lines are tacked to the tail of a paragraph of which
they form no part.   Besides all this; his lordship never again
meets with the same impertinence, which is thrust forward, on
entering the province, exactly in the same hot haste manifested
in the *Travels*.   But the most remarkable feature in all these,
and some other suspected entries, is—they seem to give a color,
in some instances scarce perceptible, in corroboration of certain
incidents recorded in the *Travels*, and which we have given

good reasons to be fabrications. In the official and other accounts there was not the shadow of a sentiment to support these extraordinary occurrences, and yet we find a sort of desideratum in the very place it would be least of all expected. Indeed, from a due consideration of his lordship's journal; and from a due consideration of all the circumstances attending the disputed entries, we are satisfied that improper liberties have been taken with it, whether sanctioned by authority or not. This much is certain; the journal, in question, was in the possession of Mr. Barrow, who made it public property. He had therefore the opportunity, and it was his interest to make any alteration he considered proper. With this remark we leave our readers to their own reflections.

OPPORTUNITIES FOR INFORMATION.

Before we conclude, there is yet another subject deserving of a few remarks :—the opportunities possessed by the gentlemen of the embassy for information.

The reader of the *Travels*, as well as the *Auto*, must necessarily observe how much the comptroller is at home among so strange a people as the Chinese. From first to last, he is never at a loss. Besides wandering about at will, he has acquired a knowledge of the language sufficient to render the presence of an interpreter supererogatory; and no other gentleman of the embassy, not even the ambassador himself, has been so caressed by the uncertain dame. "A short residence in the imperial palace of Yuen-min-yuen, a greater share of liberty than is usually permitted to strangers in this country, with the assistance of some little knowledge of the language, afforded me the means of collecting the facts and observations which I now lay before the public."

After this, it is no wonder we found our hero cutting such a conspicuous figure at Yuen-min-yuen, where, the very morning of his arrival, and before his friend Diodati appeared, he settled a multiplicity of business; stipulated for Chinese servants,(*oo*) and put his house in order. Frequently with the old eunuch we find him closeted in private, holding their little *tête-à-têtes*, as familiar as two old cronies. On the homeward journey we find him shooting across the country to make his observations, and collect his facts; traversing through fields, and getting into conversation with intelligent farmers, and such like. All this sounds somewhat strange in the ears of common sense, which struggles in vain to conjecture how the gift of tongues was acquired, and particularly after reading the observations we are about to quote from the work of Sir George Staunton.   On the first arrival, of the embassy, in the country, the difficulty of exchanging sentiment with the natives was keenly felt : interpreters were at a premium, and the whole strength of this body was then mustered with the following result :

" There was so much employment for the Chinese interpreter that a trial was now made of the skill of two persons belonging to the embassy, to whom the Chinese missionaries had endeavored to communicate some knowledge of their language, ever since they had left Naples together, above a year before.   One of these persons applied to this study with the uninterrupted diligence of mature age, but had the mortification of finding that as yet he could scarcely understand a word of what was said to him by these new comers, to whom his pronunciation was equally unintelligible ; while the other, a youth, who certainly took less pains, but whose senses were more acute, and whose organs were more flexible, proved already a tolerably good interpreter." (I, p. 489.)

Master Staunton, then, was the only individual of the embassy who could make an attempt at speaking the language, and the only other that had applied to the study of it, although an able linguist in other respects, was incapable of either understanding or being understood, after more than a year's uninterrupted diligence.   If Mr. Barrow had studied the language with success—how was he overlooked in this important trial of skill?   The author of his good fortune was only too glad of the opportunity of recording the abilities of the deserving pupil to have treated him with such neglect.   The reason, indeed, is not difficult to divine.   A very little stretch of fancy only is necessary to perceive the lamentable position of that man whose lot it is to be thrown among a strange people with language and manners as opposite to his own as the poles are assunder.   By pointing to a watch, or any article around him, the name may be acquired, if the intona-

tions of the voice are understood, and a tolerable stock of
such ideas may soon be laid in; but when he comes to
other parts of speech—a distressing difficulty immediately en-
sues which long and anxious application only can remove. The
name of an article, with a motion or two of the fingers, and
perhaps of the head, constitute the only medium of conversation; and thus were the gentlemen of the embassy situated,
unless when a missionary was present, and even then they
were under surveillance. They had all picked up their little
vocabulary of nouns, which, together with their whole tactics
in " signs," proved of very little avail nevertheless; and so far
from indulging in the *free-and-easy* style of the comptroller,
their situation was too serious a matter with Dr. Dinwiddie,
who thus laments the difficulties by which they were surrounded.

" In all our operations, no regular orders have been given;
at least, adhered to. Our *only* interpreter, an ignorant,
bigotted priest, without an atom of science, without curiosity
or liberality, puts questions frequently different from the
intentions of the proposer, either through ignorance or
prejudice. We pass through the country like so many dumb
persons, having no opportunity of asking, or receiving, information on the most common subjects."

Again: " The embassy to me is ended. Its object was
noble! the extension of commerce, and the improvement of
science. With regard to the first object—nothing that looks
like an improvement has, as yet, taken place; and as to the
other object—little could be done in a country where, while
at Pekin, we were prisoners, and on our journey hurried
forward, with hardly time to look at an object. To travel
through a fine country; to see pagodas, canals, and manu-
facturing towns, without being able to ask a single question,
is extremely mortifying. To be conducted to the bottom of
the Linho, by a colao of the empire; to receive a present
from the emperor, at parting, and the colao's farewell speech,
without knowing a word he said, and consequently to fall into
numberless blunders in our attempts to reply—what inform-

ation could we derive respecting the arts and sciences in a country where we could not converse with the inhabitants? With what countenance will Lord McCartney return to Europe, after his shameful treatment? No apology will satisfy! We go home: are asked what we have done! our answer— *we could not speak to the people!*"

Here are sentiments stamped with the impressions of honesty, and which point to a very different state of things than the miserable flourishes of the comptroller. Not only the beginning, but the termination of the embassy furnishes satisfactory testimony that *we could not speak to the people!* What influence, then, could a knowledge of the language exercise in collecting the facts " which were laid before the public?" It cannot be difficult to calculate the amount of that influence, and the point of a pin will be found ample space to contain it all. As to the enviable gentleman, in after years, persisting in his " inveterate hatred of idleness" till he acquired sufficient instruction in the Chinese hieroglyphics— so as to draw up a long flashy comment thereon — the difficulty would not be great under the auspices of an intimate friend well acquainted with the language, and who had contributed more information on the subject than Mr. Barrow was allowed to acknowledge.

RETROSPECT.

The "quarto" at last is closed, and we are done with our disagreeable task, believing another instance cannot be desired to the *black catalogue*, now dragged from this sink of iniquity.(*pp*) Nevertheless, with all this " imperfection on his head," the literary Goliah has the brazen impudence to attack, and to attempt to correct the errors of other writers, but chiefly a humble individual of the embassy, on whom the phial of indignation is emptied. This humble individual, untutored in the secrets of compilation, had not cunning enough to shut his eyes to passing events, and, unfortunately, saw some of the plague spots of the mission. In consequence of this unpardonable offence, he is branded as having no claims to credibility. That Anderson has fallen into errors is beyond doubt, but they are the errors of a defective judgment, or a misplaced recollection: they are neither inventions nor exaggerations to support a disgraceful prejudice, nor to render himself conspicuous in the eyes of his readers. The whole of his narrative carries the most indubitable impressions of honesty, a character for which the *Travels* are searched in vain.(*qq*) If ever a work was " vamped up," it is the bloated volume from which our eyes have been just relieved. Through vanity, or a love of the marvellous, other writers may have exaggerated, and even invented, but it would be difficult, we think, to find another guilty of an accumulation of such " prodigious" feats as the following list, which we combine for the cogitations of the curious.

1st.—An engraving is seen and referred to before it existed, and before it was known it would exist.

2nd.—Two distant places are seen and occupied at the same time.

3rd.—A country is seen and described as having two surfaces.

4th.—The same country is seen and described though lying beyond the reach of sight.

5th.—Another country is travelled all over before the traveller set foot in it.

6th.—The feet of women are seen and described though screened behind impenetrable bodies.

7th.—The same women are described as having the nose upon the forehead.

8th.—Ships are described as sailing over lofty mountains where no water-way existed.

All these, and a host of similar abominations, whether oversights, or whether intentional, or the result of reckless folly, are, nevertheless, justified, to the very letter, by the "facts and observations" which are the object of this inquiry. Lest, however, the reader should have any misgivings in the matter, we submit another series of "vampings," the undeniable produce of the "powerful motive," and to which we not only invite attention, but challenge the ablest flatterers of the baronet to match or confute.

1st.—*As a youthful prodigy*—our author had not only acquired the experience of, but was actually a man over twenty, before he had reached his fifteenth year.

2nd.—*As a man of stratagem*—he has contrived to appear in a procession at the moment he was busy in a palace, several miles away.

3rd.—*As an astronomer*, acquainted with such grand machines—he has calculated and described the consequences of an eclipse which nature, herself, ignores.

4th.—*As a man of science*—he has seen and described, upon the Grand canal, a contrivance which the engineer was unconscious of placing there.

5th.—*As a surveyor*—he has estimated the gardens of Yuen-min-yuen at four miles diameter, and upon the same data, without further experience, he has enlarged that estimate to ten miles in diameter, or more than nine times their former extent.

6th.—*As an arithmetician*—he has calculated the same pedestrian feat, from the same data, at a thousand miles, and also at one-tenth of thirteen hundred miles.

7th.—*As a journalist*—he has confuted the very existence of the cities he delineated with the greatest accuracy upon the map of his travels.

8th.—*As a collector of facts*—he has laid hold of a rash assertion, and spread it as the experience of an intelligent commander to illustrate a tremendous gale. He has subsequently rebuked that officer for making the assertion, without apologising for his own iniquity in disseminating it.

9th.—*As a man of shrewd observation*—he has witnessed a deeply-rooted disease cured, and a fellow mortal rescued from pain to joy, in the twinkling of an eye.

10th.—*As a man of keen observation*—he has seen the Chinese potentate sitting in a sedan chair, at the same moment he saw him sitting in a clumsy state chariot, that travelled behind that chair.

11th.—*As a man of adventure*—he has encountered one of the most tumultuous eddies on the surface of this wide world: he has been tossed over this fathomless abyss, at the same moment he was anchored and riding quietly in seventeen fathoms.

12th.—*As a traveller in a strange land*—he has been stopped and laughed at every moment, even branded as a foreign devil, yet never was insulted.

13th.—*As an author of veracity*—he has repeated statements which he averred would be idle to repeat: he has contradicted and improved those statements, which he affirmed were detailed with elegance and accuracy.

14th.—*As an invalid*—he has suffered severely for several days, though cured and put all right in twenty-four hours.

15th.—*As an old foolish man*—he has called in a physician

when he did not call in a physician, simply, because he did not require a physician.

Who, after this, could doubt the claims of John Barrow, Esq., as a fit and proper person to be placed on the British embassy ? Who could doubt his superior abilities to bring home useful and interesting information on all subjects connected with China ? And yet, alas ! to what purpose have these gifts been bestowed. Beyond performing every variety of staggering feat, for his own selfish immortality, he has passed through China and left the world as ignorant as before. Candidly, we confess, the silence of the *do-nothings* is indicative of " good sense ; " if they have not astonished natives, they have buried their ignorance in oblivion.(*rr*)

But—we fancy we hear our judges calling out—but was not John Barrow, Esq., honored with a fellowship of the Royal Society ? and is not the Royal Society a body of learned men, *enrolled under the banners of truth ?* And was not John Barrow, Esq., also honored by the College Council of Edinburgh with the highest approbation it can confer on ingenious men ? And is not the College Council of Edinburgh another learned association, *equally interested in the cause of truth ?*(*ss*) And was not John Barrow, Esq., flattered by the conductors of the *Encyclopœdia Britannica* as " an individual of acknowledged eminence in science and literature ? " And is not the *Encyclopœdia Britannica* a national work *devoted to the diffusion of truth ?* And have not learned commentators, and learned biographers, in plenty, bowed at the shrine of the literary colossus, and spread his fame ? Is not all this wonderful ? We answer—it is wonderful ! but wonders never cease ! We recommend a little fresh air, and another perusal of this small volume, when, we promise, their minds shall be at rest.

CONCLUSION

It would be a great waste of time, if it were practicable, to follow the successful baronet through all the inconsistencies of this—"the most interesting episode in the history of a prolonged life." The subject is seemingly inexhaustible; but, so far as examples were wanted, we are fully persuaded the investigation is overdone, and, in consequence, we draw it to a conclusion, with the following remarks.

During the compilation of the official account, Mr. Barrow, a vain young man, would, as chief coadjutor, receive an insight into the nature of such compilations, and, at the same time, acquire a deal of information that was never dreamed of on the embassy. He saw how a few trifling incidents could be colored to any shade, or magnified to any extent; and how easy it was to supply the place of others which had never happened. The field was unlimited, with no real obstacle to prevent him travelling through China a second time. This, no doubt, suggested the idea of making a trial upon his own account. As a matter of consequence, his reading and conversation would be prosecuted in earnest, and every available source ransacked for materials, which would open up new views, or give a stronger bias to former leanings. Thus, with his own flying visit as a basis, he laid upon the stocks the fabric which eventually usurped the name of "Travels in China." Encouraged by the example of Sir George Staunton, and flushed by his own South-African adventures, he no longer hesitated in launching his second bark upon the sea of public opinion. To judge from appearances, nothing pretending to interest has been omitted that could by any means be wrought in as information garnered by himself on the English mission. In support of the views ultimately arrived at, a host of observation, description, and anecdote, is brought forward; but we have already shown on what baseless, and also on what slippery foundations many of them are reared. Even if their authenticity were not suicidal; and even if they defied the shafts of external testimony, these illucidating occurrences are far from being satisfactory. Their very profusion is significant; and so is the dress in which they are almost universally arrayed. It is significant, too, that a solitary occasion should be made a rule to judge a population said to exceed three hundred millions. With barely an exception, a similar incident is never twice encountered; always one, *sui generis:* and besides, he never meets with an incident on the other side of the question. Had we, like the *reviewers*, trusted in the " good sense," and in the "faithful record" of the " Travels in China," we could not have resisted the belief that there must have been some complicity in the elements, themselves, the presiding deities, or what you will, in bringing about a train of coincidences, so graphic, and, altogether, so favorable, that our author, himself, could not have ordered them to better purpose. All this is significant. Then there is the abruptness with which they either commence or terminate, and the clumsiness they assume when an attempt is made to join them to the even tenor of the narrative, which ever bulges out on some side or other. But when to all this is added the damning facts, disclosed in this analysis, we cannot believe a doubt will remain on the mind of any honest reader, that one of the most disgraceful of literary impositions has been practised upon the world. All this is the more lamentable seeing nothing has been added to the stock of knowledge: with all the comptroller's exertions, to execute something on the embassy, he has only repeated what was already before the public. When, indeed, the mass of information, that now swells the detested volume, has been restored to its original sources, the remainder,

divested of jaundiced speculations, will scarcely suffice to prevent the outward bindings from clashing.

But again : admitting all these incidents to have been
merely exaggerations of stubborn fact, we have still to observe
—the reckless blundering in dates, in calculations, and other
particulars; the headstrong contradictions of the official
narrative, of his own narrative, and of the maps he constructed
with such care, are so many evidences of our author's disregard
of truth. His partiality for poetical illustration, for humour,
marvel, and remarkable expression, only throws additional
weight into the same scale; but, while confirming the low
estimate in which truth was held, it proves, in the clearest
manner, that the darling object of the "large quarto" was
amusement, squeezed from every variety of extravagant
information that could be thrust into it. The palpable
parodies, too, on his lordship, as well as the veil that has
been thrown over certain proceedings of the embassy, show a
subserviency to the powers that be, and a desire to conceal the
truth : even the conceit and egotism that is everywhere thrust
in upon the reader betray an improper sense of the great virtue.
Every circumstance, indeed, teems with significance, and points
to the *animus* that directed the pen in the compilation of the
"Travels in China : "—a work which the *Monthly* considered
might be "read with pleasure and instruction if read with
caution; "—which the *Edinburgh* considered as "adding to
the growing reputation of the author; "—which the *Anti-jacobin*
considered a "valuable addition to the splendid work of
Sir George Staunton ; "—and which the *Analytical* considered
the "best book of Travels of the age : "—but which, in our
humble opinion, is best defined as a *great humbug*. It is the
work of inordinate vanity attempting, by an indirect and
unpractical method, to bolster up prejudices, and claim the
merit of existing information : the work, in short, of an author
who had no just sense of the obligations of truth, so revered
by all well-regulated minds. From beginning to end a single
statement cannot be relied on, unless corroborated by other

testimony : assertions resting on his authority alone are utterly worthless. It may be questioned if the whole compass of travels, ancient and modern, could produce another work, claiming to be authentic, which has been nevertheless conceived and carried out in the regions of fiction accompanied by so much impossibility, absurdity, or nonsense.(*tt*) Such are *our* "unbiassed conclusions," and such are *our* foundations for them ; and these we now place in the hands of the only judges from whose decision there is no appeal. Awaiting that decision with confidence, we take our leave in the language of Dr. Johnson : " The feelings of that man is little to be envied, whose courage would not gather strength on the plains of Marathon, or whose piety would not grow warmer amid the ruins of Iona." What could the great moralist have observed on the feelings of that man who, usurping the robes of ever-adorable truth, has prostituted them to the vile purpose of imposing on his fellow men ?

FINIS.

GEORGE PHILIP AND SON, PRINTERS, LONDON AND LIVERPOOL.

NOTES.

(a) While the yet undistinguished son of obscure, humble parents is weaving his name with an "Esq." we find the son of Sir Francis Baring, Bart., rises no higher in dignity than a simple "Mr."

(b) After hitting right and left, in moving past, the *Auto* again looks back with a contemptuous glance upon the *do-nothings*, and sums up their united abilities, thus : "Before the embassy left England it was generally understood that great pains had been taken in the selection of the gentlemen who had the good fortune to be included in the suite of the ambassador. The brief description that I have here given does not exactly correspond with such a notion. If I except the able and interesting account of the proceedings and result of the British embassy by the late Sir George Staunton, nothing of a scientific, physical, ethical, or ethnical, character appeared from any of them." (p. 52.) All this may be true; still we are of opinion that our author has not followed the wholesome advice of scripture," " Judge not, that ye be not judged." We are very much mistaken if our readers do not agree in this opinion before the enquiry be finished.

(c) Some writers on China are impressed with the idea that Mr Barrow was at liberty to move about the capital, but this is a great mistake, resulting from the implicit confidence placed in his assertions.

(d) An author struggling against his convictions must feel in a very awkward position, particularly when he has reason to believe he will be suspected. Such is the position of Sir George Staunton, who, while conscious of the folly, is, never-theless, driven by his infatuation to endeavor to change the aspect of the treat-ment experienced by the embassy at the capital ; and the consequence is a woful accumulation of unintelligible discrepancies. When measured by the standard of others, equally in a position to judge, these discrepancies assume an intelligible but most disreputable aspect. Before the ambassador started into Tartary, we find " His excellency rode in an English carriage, drawn by four Tartar horses ;" but, on applying to the journal of that nobleman, he is unconscious of having done any such thing; and he is justified by Anderson, who fully explains the matter.

"While the ambassador continued in Pekin," we also read, " Some of the gentlemen had occasion often to pass from thence to the imperial palace in the country, and returning at different times through different suburbs, gates, and streets, had opportunities of viewing most parts of the capital." (II. p. 164.) Mr. Barrow is the only individual who can represent the gentlemen, in question, and, answering for himself in the extract above, he gives a flat denial by affirming that *we* were accustomed to pass through one gate only.

Again : " The gentlemen were very handsomely treated in the palace." (II. p. 319.) If so, one of the handsomely treated gentlemen replies " The keeper of the hall of audience was the most capricious creature in the world ; being some-times extremely civil and communicative ; sometimes sullen, and not deigning to open his lips : and whenever he took it into his head to be offended, he was sure to practice some little revenge. The quality, and quantity of our dinner generally depended on the state of his humour." "The great number of these creatures about the palace made my residence there extremely disagreeable." (p. 232.)

What must Sir George Staunton have thought of the *Travels* had he been spared to read such contradictions? To be thus continually opposed to the daggers of all other witnesses is bad enough ; but to find the well-beloved, the kindly-treated whom he had raised from obscurity among the conspirators, might justly wring from his bleeding bosom, *Et tu Brute !*

(e) The reader has only to refer to Lord McCartney's journal in proof of this.

(f) The date of this eclipse is taken from Dr. D's journal, and is confirmed to a minute by the highest authority in the land, thus :

Royal Observatory, Greenwich,
London, S. E.
1860, August 14.

Sir,

The times of the lunar eclipse of 1793, August 21. (a partial eclipse of 8¾ digits on the S. limb), in Greenwich mean solar time, were as follows :

		h. m.
Beginning	. . . . .	1. 29.
Middle	. . . . . .	2. 52.
End	. . . .	4. 16.

Adopting 7h. 47m. as the eastern longitude of Pekin, the Pekin times are :

		h. m.
Beginning	. . . . .	9. 16.
Middle	. . . . . .	10. 39.
End	. . . .	12. 3.

I am, Sir, your obedient servant,
G. B. Airy.

W. J. Proudfoot, Esq.

(g) The procession to Pekin here so pompously set forth, though equally answerable for our purpose, is a gross misrepresentation of the fact, and shows the little reliance that is to be placed on even one statement : there was, in fact, no order of procession arranged, or at least adhered to, as the various parties pushed ahead, or lingered behind, as they thought proper. But respecting the heavy articles that paraded in front—they were not in the disorderly procession at all. They were marched off by degrees on the previous day ; and by degrees reached their destination, at Hungyayuen, the day after the arrival of the embassy, apparently travelling through Pekin by a different route.

(h) The orthography of Chinese names is deplorable ; we have, however, sub-stituted Nanyang for the Nansheun of the *Travels*, and for the Nanchoo of Lord McCartney's journal, believing it to be more appropriate.

(*i*) "At an early hour of the morning," observes Anderson, "The baggage was put on board the junks, with a regularity, as well as despatch, that cannot well be described. There was a sufficient depth of water in this river to bring the junks close to the quay; so that the coolies, of which there were a great number, acting under the orders of the mandarine and his servants, and guarded by soldiers, soon transferred every article that belonged to the embassy on board the vessels to which it was specifically assigned." "About eleven o'clock the suite were all on board, and the whole fleet ready for sailing. We accordingly renewed our voyage, and began it by passing under a wooden bridge of seven arches," &c. (p. 240.)

The sailing of the vessels on December 11, and the objects seen that day, as described by Anderson, is quite corroborated by Lord McCartney's journal, which carries the additional importance of having been published under the authority of Barrow.

(*j*) That it is a fabrication is evident from the clashing statements, and it is all but confirmed from the following admission: "When the new viceroy of Canton understood from our conductors that the English found great pleasure in walking and looking about them, he immediately gave orders that the gentlemen in the train of the ambassador should walk whenever they pleased without any molestation." (p. 527.)

We are assured this order was issued previous to the occurrence in question; how, then, would any officer dare to disobey such authority, or lay himself open to punishment and degradation? But every inquiry into its place on the journey only tends to strengthen the same belief. Speaking of the incident, Sir George Staunton observes the gentlemen were "once" rudely interrupted; and Mr. Barrow, "that the viceroy of Canton was then with the embassy:" such is the scope carved out by the incident-mongers. It appears from the former, however, that exercises on the banks took place only when the embassy was retarded; and the incident in question is introduced to the reader's notice when descending the Lonshiaton, as near as possible after passing the city of Quangsin. At that juncture, the barges were carried forward with a full flowing tide in their favor, and where no shallows impeded their progress: At that juncture, too, Mr. Barrow, after opening the floodgates of heaven, has swelled the river to an "enormous size," scattering destruction in all directions. Whatever opportunities may have occurred in other places for such exercises, none presented themselves on the downward passage of this river, which was too accommodating for the journey, while the weather was too gloomy to step ashore. A distinguishing feature of the Staunton-Barrow school is to keep dates and localities of incidents carefully out of sight, and every attempt to fix on either only clashes with some other details. No person, notwithstanding, ever studied to better purpose the art of generalizing and confounding than Sir George Staunton, who, with the skill of a master, could avoid seeing what was before his eyes without exciting suspicion; or see what was impossible to be seen, without committing himself. His incidents and anecdotes, as a whole, are so well arranged that it is only through the ungovernable pupil, vaunting his own prowess, that the weak point is ascertained, and the stronghold rendered pregnable.

(*k*) The hint for the present illustration is, like the last, borrowed from the official volumes, and is merely the following paragraph dressed up in our author's best style:

"A sufficient number of men were impressed by the mandarines to track the boats; but the pay allowed by government was not adequate to the labor, and many of them withdrew from the task whenever they found an opportunity of escaping unperceived. It often happened that a set of trackers were exchanged in the night, that fresh might be surprised and forced into the service. A superintendent, like a negro driver in the West Indies, marches generally behind them with a whip, to quicken their pace and prevent their desertion." (II, p. 379.)

Thus, occurrences said to have transpired on the Euho, after being outrageously overdrawn and improved by every circumstance that could be thrust into them, are presented as a universal illustration of the miserable condition of the boat-men, and the inhumanity with which they were treated. Believing inhumanity to be the offspring of every country it is quite probable that some instances occurred during the long journey; and it is equally probable that the officers had occasion to keep a sharp look out, as testified by the following example at the period in question:

"One of the trackmen had been intrusted with money to buy some articles at the last village. He went off with some clothes belonging to his companions. A person was sent after him: he was found drinking soochoo; was taken before a mandarine, and committed to prison." (Dr. D.)

(*l*) Drowning Chinese at Linsin.

(*m*) In Lord McCartney's journal there is an entry about a dismal midnight fog, at this juncture, but not a word of the upset. This entry shall yet be commented on.

(*n*) Or, if it be more agreeable to orthography, a summersault.

(*o*) Neither did the Dutch, nor subsequent English embassy take any notice of such wrecks.

(*p*) As a collector of amusing varieties, Mr. Barrow is very ready to let his readers know that Marco Polo received the epithet of Mr. Mark Million, from the sentiments he used in dictating his travels. Feeling confident the association of ideas was strongly developed in our author, it appears to us impossible for him to have overlooked the glaring fact—with how much greater propriety he might have been linked to one of his own favorite amplifications, such as "prodigious" —"enormous"—"vast." *Sir John Prodigious* would, to the eye and ear, be quite as agreeable, and certainly more appropriate than "Mr. Mark Million;" because we are in a position to test the statements of the Englishman, which was not the case with those who dubbed the Venetian traveller.

(*q*) Our author's mode of taking his laugh out of the Captain of the Hindostan is as follows:

Mr. B. "Captain, would you put into a book what you have just told me?"

Capt. M. "Perhaps not exactly in the same words."

Mr. B. "No! I am sure you would make a great reduction to the number of your drums and trumpets."

Nevertheless, without any reduction to the drums and trumpets, Mr. B. actually did what he was *sure* Capt. M. could not have the face to do—he put the extravagant assertion "into a book," in order to enlighten mankind on the fury of a typhoon. And, how surprising! these palpable and abominable exaggerations, as specimens of travel, hold the very "first rank in excellence."

(*r*) Confined as the gentlemen were to the boats in which they travelled— their only opportunities of "striking across the country," to examine objects, was by means of the telescope, which was in constant requisition, and the cause of occasional terror to spectators. "On presenting the three-foot telescope to a crowd, on the left bank, they all ran off, supposing it to be a gun, and being persuaded the English, the most ferocious people in the world, think nothing of killing any person they meet." (Dr. D.) This incident occurs upon the very day when the "long range" must have been sweeping the inhospitable swamps, and making the incomprehensible discoveries.

(s) In the "Preliminary Matter," our traveller apologises for his barrenness as a natural historian. "In the route of the grand inland navigation no very great variety nor number of subjects occur"—"few native plants and still fewer wild animals." (p. 6.) Nevertheless, he found the swamps and lakes absolutely teeming with subjects: in birds alone the numbers were not only "great," but the variety itself was "vast." It is presumed the missionaries were not naturalists, otherwise there would have been no dearth of subjects. Possibly, gentlemen of the Barrow-school may object to the feathered races being described as "animals;" if so, we object to "scorpions and scolopendras" being thrown into the same category.

(t) Dreary as it appeared when enveloped in its atmosphere, the land of swamps assumed a very different aspect from the summit of Mount Melin, where our traveller, while enjoying a little fresh air, was enabled to take a retrospective view of his past journey, embracing the whole at one glance of his mind's eye. Possibly the elevated position dispelled the fogs by which he had been surrounded, at all events, the country, instead of being abandoned to "cranes, herons, and guillemots," was swarming with human life; and "so great were the numbers engaged in fishing who lived entirely in floating vessels, that we judged the waters to be fully as populous as the land." (p. 557.)

But this picture is repainted on another occasion in even more forcible colors. "That part of the country over which the grand communication is effected between the two extremities of the empire, abounds with swamps and morasses where population is excessive, and where the multitudes of shipping that pass and repass create a never-failing demand for grain and other vegetable products." (p. 567.)

In forming a just estimate of a Barrow-swamp our readers will, after all, have some difficulty to contend with. Whether the population was "excessive," or whether abandoned to "cranes, herons, and guillemots," will necessarily depend upon the mode of interpreting the various aspects in which these swamps were seen by their great discoverer.

(u) Dr. Abel decidedly states that the canal was neither carried through any hill, nor over any valley.

(v) According to this description there are *only* three rivers of note in all China. Of these the Euho, itself, although a "great river" on the present, is but a "small river" on another occasion. Camelion-like, the "facts and observations" will change their colors agreeably to the whim floating uppermost in the brains of their author. But the details of the Authentic Account, which B. informs us are "so elegant and so accurate" that it would be idle in any one to attempt improving thereon, affirm that "many and great rivers run through the several provinces of China." It even invests the Chentang with this attribute.

(w) Among the abominations of the *Travels* the sheer nonsense, arising from an ignorance of grammatical construction, is not the least remarkable. However learned in the Latin and Chinese languages, the "able scholar" has made sad havoc with his own; but as this arises from other causes than the "powerful motive," it does not properly come within the sphere of this investigation. Nevertheless, having just quoted a sentence to the purpose, the following specimen will suffice : Describing the Chinese beauties, the " learned linguist" *places the nose on the middle of the forehead !*

(*x*) It was once our lot to visit the town of Dundee where—inquiring for a certain gentleman—we were civilly asked, in return, if he was a " *wise-like man.*" Confounded for a moment at such an unexpected Yankeeism, we begged an explanation of the expression, which proved to be in very general use for a stout, well-fed looking person. Amused at the idea, we have, often since, pointed out to ourselves *wise-like men*, and *wise-like things*, and among others the official volumes of the McCartney embassy, to which the expression applies with great justice.

(*y*) It is not a little remarkable that, while attempting to assimilate his Poosa of the Quangsin souterrain to his " intelligent mother," the author of the *Travels* should, in reality, admit Poosa to be the most monstrous divinity in all China. This he illustrates from the specimen seen by Van Braam which was "ninety feet high, having four heads and forty-four arms." (p. 471.) If Mr. B. was desirous to clothe his Shingmoo in the garb of a Poosa, why not do it in a business-like manner?

(*z*) The subsequent English embassy, which found the deity removed, proved, both by their drawings and descriptions of the temple, that there were only two stories.

(*aa*) Recent writers on China have generally looked upon the *Travels* as valuable authority, and, among others, Sir John Davis, while acknowledging their assistance in this respect, regards them as holding the first rank in " date and excellence." In his work, " The Chinese," the gardens of Yuen-min-yuen are wholly elucidated from the experience of Mr. Barrow, who is said to estimate their contents at " about twelve square miles," notwithstanding the *Travels* have fixed them at something like a hundred square miles, or about sixty thousand acres. Now, the author of "The Chinese" either did not comprehend the meaning of the borrowed language, or he does Mr. Barrow great injustice. He knew Mr. Barrow had given in two estimates, the first a hasty one, no doubt, before it could be tested by the experience of subsequent travellers ; and if Sir John Davis has adopted that one, he has not only imposed upon his readers, but, as observed, done great injustice to the comptroller, who corrected the rough draught at the first opportunity.

The pertinacity, indeed, with which some commentators cling to Barrow as an authority, even when the particular fact has been exploded, is not a little remarkable. The same learned author of " The Chinese" continues to adopt, in all their integrity, the Barrow-swamps of the Poyang, although he had occular demonstration to the contrary on the west side of the lake, where, besides the picturesque mountains, the very shores, instead of reeds and rank grasses, were, like those of the sea, covered with " shingles." Entering the lake from the south-east, the Rev. Dr. Milne found the country not only under cultivation, but the lake itself so well defined as to be fifteen feet deep at the very edge.

(*bb*) While pouring out his rancour upon "one Eneas Anderson " our author generally spills the greater part upon himself, though affecting not to see it. For instance—he looks with astonishment on the " exaggerated accounts" which the "vamped up" volume gives of the population, and yet he, himself, more than confirms those exaggerated accounts—the population being "excessive," " vast," or " immense," as occasion requires. But let us see the result of a little reasoning on the matter. If the population of the swamps was eventually found to be " excessive ; " and if the population of every part of the province of Kiangnan was " vast ; " and, further, if the population of every part of the province Chekiang was " immense "—What, intelligent reader ! must have been the state of that part of the country between Hanchoo and Nimpo, a distance of some hundred and thirty miles, which was " by far the most populous in the whole "journey ?" Would anything short of " a country full of houses," (the Irishman's definition of London) satisfy the conditions ? Is there anything in Eneas Anderson to match this ?

(*cc*) The *Auto* accompanies its description of the glacis with a profile or section of the contrivance, as it appeared on the Grand canal ; so anxious is the " powerful motive," to elucidate one of its most important facts.

It may possibly interest some of our readers to learn that the owner of the " motive," which manufactured the glacis for the Grand canal, took credit to himself for being " father of the Royal Society." Something more than ordinary, it is true, might have been expected from such a personage, but who, in the name of goodness, could have calculated on such a specimen of engineering skill ?

Shade of Sir H. Davy, and other illustrious confederates ! have your brilliant investigations then fraternized with those of a "motive" which discovered a glacis where none existed ; which witnessed an eclipse that never happened ; and which illustrated a typhoon by the rash assertion of an individual who did not believe in his own words ? Is it come to this—is the author of such unearthly discoveries—of such disreputable illustrations, allowed to subscribe himself a "fellow"—yea ! the " father" of a society which unfurled the banners of truth, and gathered immortal honors in her name ?

(*dd*) Even Dr. Abel is unwilling to wander from his path in search of "facts and observations," and yet it appears to us that he undertook his work expressly to depreciate the Chinese. His disappointments and sufferings in the country, and no less the wreck of the Alceste, had their due influence upon a temperament easily offended, and induced him to retaliate upon unoffending and even inanimate objects.

(*ee*) The late Daniel O'Connell, Esq., used to consider his own countrymen as forming the finest peasantry in the world.

(*ff*) The disposition to ignore information, in its legitimate place, on purpose to produce it on some prior or subsequent occasion, may not always excite suspicion when it is merely an incidental occurrence which could happen at one place or time as well as another ; but the effect is sometimes rather awkward when it has relation to fixed periods, or immovable objects. For instance, the embassy, on its arrival at Hungyayuen, passed through a town called Hatien. No sensible traveller, who had the use of his eyes, and wished to see the town, would have shut his eyes on such an occasion ; nevertheless Mr. Barrow wanted to see it, and yet he passed through without seeing it. However, exactly five days afterwards, when the embassy returned to Pekin, and passed again through this town, we find Mr. Barrow, notwithstanding he is several miles away, attending to other duties, has contrived not only to appear in the procession, but with open eyes, he there and then discovers that he " passed through the great street of a town called Hatien," and in consequence introduces it to edify his readers.

(*gg*) It is inconceivable how Sir George Staunton, who was in hot pursuit attentions to the embassy, on the part of his imperial majesty, should overlook the " Card of happiness," the strongest mark of friendship and affection which the Chinese potentate could send to the King of England. The baronet knew the nature of a " eujoy," and admits, though in a suspicious manner, that the ambassador received something of the kind ; but nothing more. On what ground then can his silence of the emperor's regard for the King of England be defended ?   Is the smell of the great manufactory not palpable ?

(*hh*) Since writing the above, we have seen an account of the Amherst embassy by Dr. Abel, who reconciles the inconsistencies of the Barrow and Ellis visits on the ground that the pagoda had been repaired in the mean time. Dr. Abel, however, with all the prestige of his name, has not made a very *able* apology for such palpable contradictions. With equal propriety might he have accounted for the alterations on the west side of the Poyang lake, which, at the time of the Barrow-visit, was very different from what the subsequent travellers found it.   If any reliance is to be placed on the "facts and observations" of Mr. Barrow ; and if the Chinese improved the pagoda at Linsin, after his visit, by the introduction of a staircase and deities, there is no rule in reason to prevent the Chinese improving the scenery of the Poyang, by the introduction of highly picturesque mountains.

(*ii*) Amidst a flourish of biblical quotations, with now and then a thrust at irreligion, our author holds up to sweet contemplation the picture of a laboring peasant discharging his Sunday duties to his God, and "rubbing of the dust of the week." In doing so, he exultingly inquires into the feelings of that man who could not participate in the peasant's serenity of mind. This is excellent, Mr. Barrow ! but in return let us inquire into the feelings of that man who, while painting this pious picture, nevertheless, dips his pencil in the impious colors so profusely spread not only throughout the entire *Travels*, but the *Auto* itself—the sweet child of his gray hairs.

(*jj*) In describing the Grand canal, the reader has already seen some of the beauties resulting from the combined efforts of "All the talents :" when applied to measure the length of this great work, the same efforts produce results no less exquisite. His lordship and the comptroller have discovered that the distance from the Euho to the Yellow river is two hundred miles, or thereabouts, notwithstanding Sir George Staunton "put it into a book" that it was two hundred miles to the summit level only, which a glance at the map shows is not one-third of the distance to the Yellow river. Thus the same two points, which are fixed, by the former, at two hundred miles apart, would, by the proportion of the latter, exceed six hundred miles. And what is no less edifying, the baronet, after measuring the total length of the Canal from the Euho to Hanchoo, finds it is no more than five hundred miles, or thereabouts, a distance which would neither bring him to the Yellow river, nor half way along the Canal. Mr. B., himself, is in no better a "fix" although, by a different scale we presume, he finds the canal between the same extreme points to be six hundred miles long—a hundred more than the baronet found it. The Yellow river divides the canal somewhere towards the middle, but makes the southern division rather shorter than the northern one. In defiance of this fact, Mr. B. estimates the southern division at four hundred miles, and the northern, or larger one, at no more than two hundred miles—the lesser distance just double the length of the greater. Who could believe that the author of a treatise on a case of mathematical drawing instruments could make such a use of a scale and a pair of compasses.

(*kk*) If the pilots really committed a great blunder in mistaking one bay for another it should be borne in mind that the place was many hundred miles away, and that they had not seen it for many years ; and besides they were forced upon a service which they did not undertake to accomplish. Remembering all this, their ignorance of the coast may partly be apologised for ; but what is to apologise for an author who, sitting quietly at ease, with time and every opportunity to write an intelligible narrative, nevertheless, beats the pilots on their own ground—stupidity ! Those who cast reflections should take care that they are not in the position of the man in the glass house (*ll*) The *Auto*, which is generally the most honest of the two, confirms the account of the elder brother, in language that leaves no room for a doubt: "It occupied us seven days against the stream to reach its source, not far from the only city on its banks of the third rank, called Tchantangshien."

(*mm*) The *Auto*, while repeating, renders the blunder more apparent by specifying the month.

(*nn*) It is surprising that this, with a long array of kindred nonsense, escaped the critical acumen of the lady who so kindly undertook to revise and correct the *Auto :* it certainly does not give us a very favourable opinion of her abilities for such a task. We even find the *Athenæum* recommending a book teeming with such trash as "a pleasant addition to the Englishman's library."

(*oo*) If instead of his "servants" our author had substituted his *keepers* the nail would have been hit on the head to the greatest nicety.

(*pp*) Twice does Mr. Barrow inform us that he has called the Poyang the "sink of China." If, instead of outraging a beautiful lake that so ill deserved it, he had stored up the euphonious sentiment as the TITLE to his *Travels*, he would for once have told the truth, and in some measure have redeemed his credit by thus acknowledging he was romancing after all.

(*qq*) In his eagerness to depreciate the labors of Anderson, the giant in reputation is careful to tell us it "was a work vamped up by a London bookseller as a speculation that could not fail," and disdainfully asks, "What dependence can be placed on the information of an author who states as a fact, that he saw tea and rice growing on the banks of the Peiho, two articles of the culture of which, in the whole province of Pechelee, they know no more than we do in England," (p. 579.) Perhaps so ; but if Anderson was in error, it was an error of judgment— an error, that, in the case of rice at least, extended to every individual of the embassy at the time. It will only be necessary to instance Captain Parish, and the super-excellent the minister plenipotentiary himself, who tells us, on the banks of the Peiho, "wheat in dry, and rice in moist, situations, were said to be cultivated to advantage." (II, p. 45.) We will not stay now to inquire "what dependence can be placed on this information," of his super-excellency, but, allowing the "dressed up" volume to fight its battles alone, shall leave in the hands of our readers the decision of this important question : the vampings of Barrow *versus* the vampings of Anderson. Take a solitary example of the former, such as the Eclipse at Tonchoo,—the Canton Ulcer,—the Glacis on the Grand Canal,—or the Keeto whirlpool, and we shall stake it against *every* error and defect, *in globo*, that can be brought against the Narrative of Eneas Anderson.

(*rr*) The reader is requested to look back to the observations and notes, respecting the *do-nothings*, at page 18 of this inquiry.

(*ss*) That every one of our readers may be assured there is no mistake in regard to the high estimation in which the author of the *Travels* was held by learned men, and particularly by the literati of Edinburgh on conferring their honorary degree of LL.D. we subjoin the announcement of Principal Baird, as published in the *Auto*.

"College, Edinburgh, January 22, 1821.
"Sir,

"I have the honor to inform you, by the command of the Senatus Academicus of the university, that, at their meeting on Saturday last, they conferred on you the honorary degree of LL.D., and they request you to believe that they have conferred the degree as a proof of their respect for your literary talents, and for your effective zeal in promoting the progress of Science. Allow me to add that in this case the *graduation* was moved by Professor Jamieson, and carried by the unanimous, warm approbation of the meeting.

"To myself, personally, I beg leave to assure you that the motion, and the mode of its receptance, afforded great pleasure.

"May you long live to enjoy these tokens of esteem, which every enlightened friend of science and of his country's honor is disposed to offer you.

"I remain, Sir,

"John Barrow, Esq."   "GEO. H. BAIRD."

The compliment hereby paid to the "powerful motive" would not have been unworthy of the discoverer of the laws of gravitation; although the *motive* to the *laws* is like the murkiness of midnight compared to the effulgence of noon day.

(*tt*) Had the *Travels* existed in the time of Burns, we should have sworn that he had just risen from their perusal when he penned the sentiment,

" Some books are lies frae end to end."

But from whatever source the poet drew his inspiration—of this we are sure—he never read, nor ever heard of a work (Pinto, the accredited prince of liars, not excepted) that more fully confirms the justness of his observation than the subject of this review.

www.ingramcontent.com/pod-product-compliance
Ingram Content Group UK Ltd.
Pitfield, Milton Keynes, MK11 3LW, UK
UKHW042153280225
455719UK00001B/305